STUDENT'S BOOK

Carol Read • Mark Ormerod

Welcome back to the Tiger Tracks Social Learning Network

Lessons 1 & 2

 **1 Listen and read.** 

Welcome back to the Tiger Tracks Social Learning Network! This year, we:

- communicate with children from different English-speaking countries
- share ideas and opinions
- learn amazing facts about the world
- learn about different cultures
- do interesting and creative projects
- prepare for secondary school

1

Hello. My name's Zoe. I come from Canada. I'm 11.

Character: sporty and artistic
Interests: the Olympic Games, athletics
Ambitions: to run in the London marathon

2

Hi there. My name's Florence. I'm from Jamaica. I'm 12 years old.

Character: scientific and creative
Interests: nutrition and cooking
Ambitions: to present a TV programme about food from around the world

 **2 Listen and repeat.**  **Say and identify.**

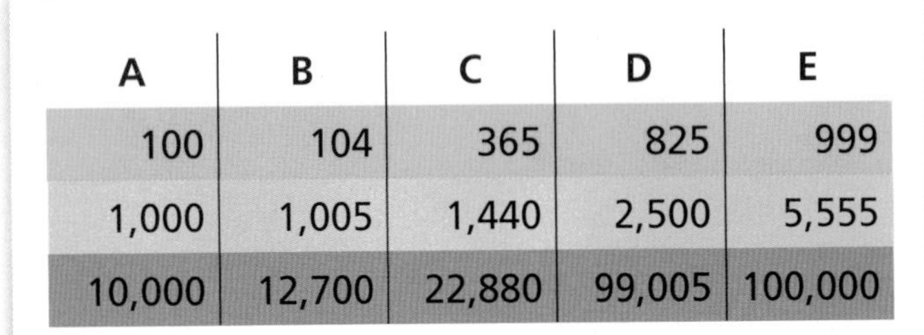

A	B	C	D	E
100	104	365	825	999
1,000	1,005	1,440	2,500	5,555
10,000	12,700	22,880	99,005	100,000

 **3 Listen and say which number.**

Why not play big numbers bingo?

3

Hi there. My name's Finn. I'm from Ireland. I'm 14 years old.

Character: artistic and imaginative
Interests: comic books, theatre and cinema
Ambitions: to write and direct a movie

4

Hello. I'm Becky. I live in England. I'm 12 years old.

Character: scientific and techy
Interests: famous scientists and inventors
Ambitions: to be a doctor and work in a hospital

5

Hello, everyone! My name's Ed. I'm from Wales. I'm 13 years old.

Character: musical and sporty
Interests: musical instruments and football
Ambitions: to play in a band and travel round the world

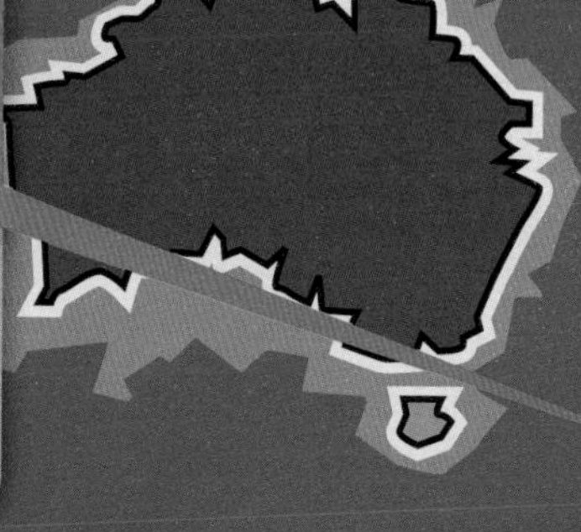

6

Hello there. I'm Scott. I live in New Zealand. I'm 12.

Character: sporty and adventurous
Interests: nature and geography
Ambitions: to learn to climb mountains

Can you find and name the countries the TTSLN visited in Tiger Time 5?

4 CD1 5 **Listen and say. Play *Who is it?***

She's creative. She's interested in cooking. She wants to present a TV programme about good food.

5 **Ask your friends. Tell the class.**

What type of person are you?

What are you interested in?

What do you want to do in the future?

1  In your free time

In this unit:

- I **name** and **talk about** free time activities.
- I **listen to** and **read** a success story *A talented boy*.
- I **talk about** what activities people like doing.
- I **find out about** Welsh and UK culture.
- I **act out** inviting a friend to a concert in a role play.
- I **read about** different languages, and **write** and **present** a project.

Lesson 1

1 Listen and say. 

Tiger Tracks SLN POST

Hi. I'm Ed. I live in Cardiff, the capital of Wales. I go to a youth club. Guess which activities I do at the club. Which activities do you do?

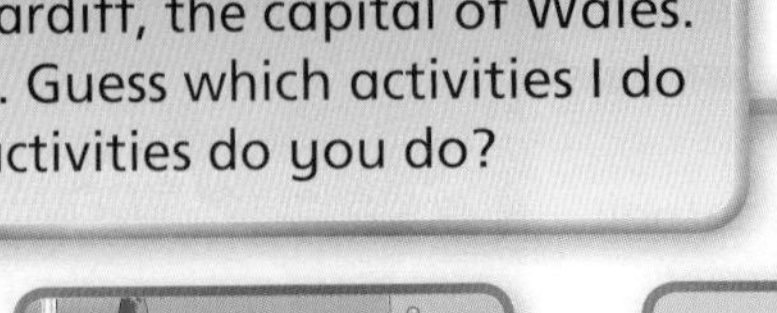

1 go to pop concerts

2 do puzzles

3 collect things

4 play the drums

5 juggle

6 use the internet

7 make things

8 play chess

9 go fishing

10 practise a foreign language

2 Listen and find out. Which activities does Ed do at the youth club? Now ask and talk about you.

Do you juggle in your free time?

Yes, I quite often do.

Yes, I sometimes do.

No, I never do.

3 Listen and do the vocabulary quiz.

To do this, you need a board but you don't need any dice. You need a king and a queen.

INTERNET TRACKS Look at a map of the UK. Find Cardiff. How far is it from Cardiff to London?

Lesson 2

4  **Listen and read.**

POST ✓

Here's some information about the youth club I go to. I think it's a great club. What do you think?

THE STREETWISE YOUTH CLUB

- Are you between 10 and 16 years old?
- Have you got lots of free time?
- Do you like doing lots of different activities?

If your answers are YES, YES, YES, then the Streetwise Youth Club is the place for you.

At the club, you can meet lots of children. And you can choose from a variety of activities.

Playing sports and games

You can play chess, cards and many other games. You can play football, table tennis and many other sports. We organise competitions with other youth clubs around the UK.

Collecting and making things

Many of our members are very creative. We collect old magazines, plastic bottles and old clothes, and we make things from these recycled objects.

Going on excursions

At the weekend, we sometimes go on excursions. We go to interesting museums and great pop concerts. We explore the countryside around our town.

Learning new skills

At the Streetwise Youth Club you can learn new computer skills. You can also practise a foreign language or learn to play a musical instrument.

READING TIP Use the headings to help you find information quickly.

The Streetwise Youth Club is open every afternoon after school and all day on Saturday.
Membership: £10 a month. You can come once a week, twice a week, or every day of the week. You choose!

5 Answer the questions.

1. How old are members of the youth club?
2. How many sports are named in the text?
3. When is the youth club open?
4. Can you go to the youth club on Sunday?
5. How much does it cost to be a member of the youth club?

6  **Work in groups. Remember and write.**

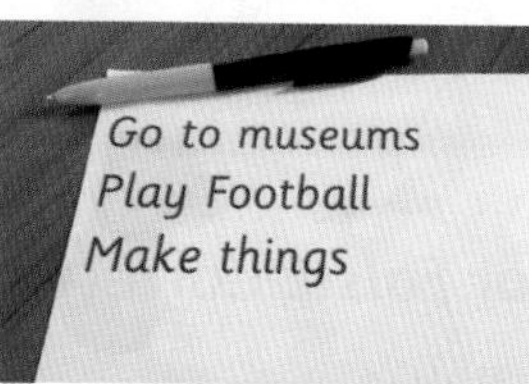

THINKING SKILLS
Remembering

TALK ABOUT IT!

7 Think and say.

I think going to a youth club is a good idea because you can meet other children.

INTERNET TRACKS Find out what you can see at the National Museum, Cardiff.

This is a success story about some people I know at the Streetwise Youth Club. I hope you like it.

POST ✓

Lesson 3

8 CD1 12 **Listen to and read the story.**

A talented boy

- **What activity is David good at?**
- **What does David's brother do?**

1

David is at the Streetwise Youth Club for the first time.

Hi there, David. My name's Tessa. Let me show you the activities you can do here.

2

Tom and Lucy like playing chess. They play together every Thursday.

Hi, Tom. Hi, Lucy.

This is Paul. He likes making things. He's very creative.

Hello, David.

3

My name's Liz and this is Benny.
We don't like playing chess or making things. We think the youth club is boring.
Oh dear.

4

David, what do you like doing?
I like dancing.
Did you hear that? He likes dancing!
That's not cool!

9 **Read and say *True* or *False*. Correct the false sentences.**

1. David joins a chess club.
2. Liz and Benny like making things.
3. David doesn't like dancing.
4. David's brother is an art teacher.
5. The children decide to form a dance group.
6. One week later the children give a performance.

Tiger Time Values
Think about it!

Is it important to try new activities? Why?

Do you like trying new activities?

5 David dances for Tessa and the other children. They are amazed.

David can stand on his hands.

He can do somersaults.

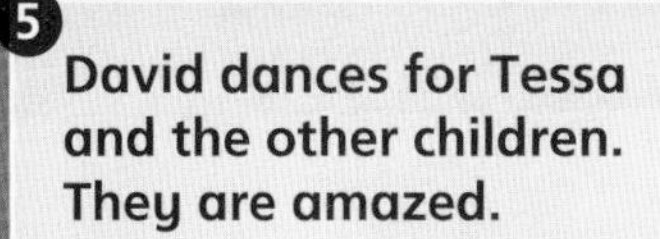

Wow!
That's amazing!
That's fantastic!

6

You're really good. I want to dance like you.
Me too!
OK. Let's form a dance group. My brother can help us. He's a dance teacher.

7 David, Liz and Benny work with David's brother. They work very hard for many months.

Jump to the left. Put your hands in the air and bend your knees.

8 One year later, the children perform in the streets of Cardiff. They are a great success.

Wow! Look at them! They're brilliant.
That's incredible.
They're fantastic.

9

Well done, David. And thank you. Because of you, Liz and Benny have got an activity they like doing.
I love dancing.
Me too. And we love going to the youth club.

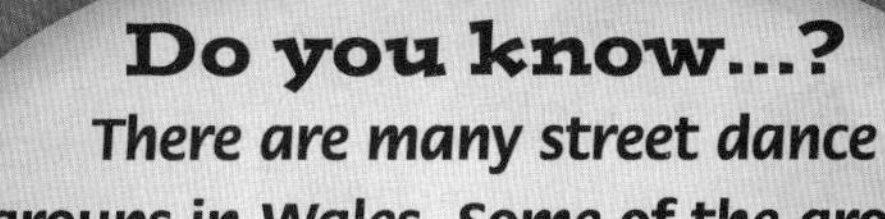

Do you know...?

There are many street dance groups in Wales. Some of the groups compete in the World Street Dancing Championship every year.

TALK ABOUT IT!

10 Ask and say.

1 Do you like the story? Why? / Why not?
2 What's your favourite part of the story?
3 Do you think it's easy to be a street-dance champion?
4 Do you like dancing?

Everyday phrases: learn and use!

Did you hear that?
That's amazing!
You're really good!
That's incredible!

GRAMMAR TRACKS

Lesson 4

11  **Listen and read. Who does more sport?**

Julia — I **like going** to the youth club.

Julia is 15 years old and she's a member of the Streetwise Youth Club. She **likes going** to the club because she can see her friends. They **like using** the club computers to do their homework. Julia **doesn't like playing** table tennis, but she sometimes plays football. And she's learning to play the drums at the club. She **loves playing** the drums.

Anthony — I think the youth club is great.

Anthony is 12. He goes to the Streetwise Youth Club with his brother every Friday after school. They **like juggling**, and **playing** board games, football and table tennis at the club. Anthony **doesn't like playing** computer games, but he **likes using** the internet to find out about science. Anthony is also learning Chinese at the club with a boy from China. He **likes learning** foreign languages.

12 **Ask and answer.**

Does Julia like juggling?

No, she doesn't.

It doesn't say.

Yes, she does.

13 **Listen, repeat and learn.** 

like* + *...ing **(revision and extension)**

I / You / We / They	like	swimming. juggling. playing chess.
He / She	likes	

I / You / We / They	don't like	swimming. juggling. playing chess.
He / She	doesn't like	

Do you	like	swimming? juggling? playing chess?	Yes,	I do.	No,	I don't.
Does he / she				he / she does.		he / she doesn't.

14 **Be a grammar detective! Look at page 7 in the AB.**

When there is a verb after *like*, what form of the verb do we use?

What are the short answers to questions beginning with *Do you like...?*

Can you find five examples of *like + ...ing* in the story?

FAST TRACK GRAMMAR *Write five sentences about what you and your family like doing.*

Lesson 5

15 CD1 16 **Listen and count the syllables. Identify the sentence stress.**

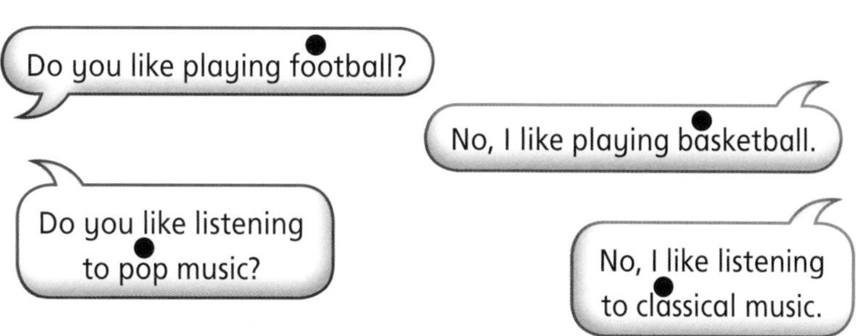

Do you like playing football?
No, I like playing basketball.
Do you like listening to pop music?
No, I like listening to classical music.

16 CD1 17 **Listen and say *True* or *False*. Correct the false sentences.**

	Julia	Sarah	Anna	Ben	Jake	Billy
☺						
☹						

17 **Play *Who am I thinking about?***

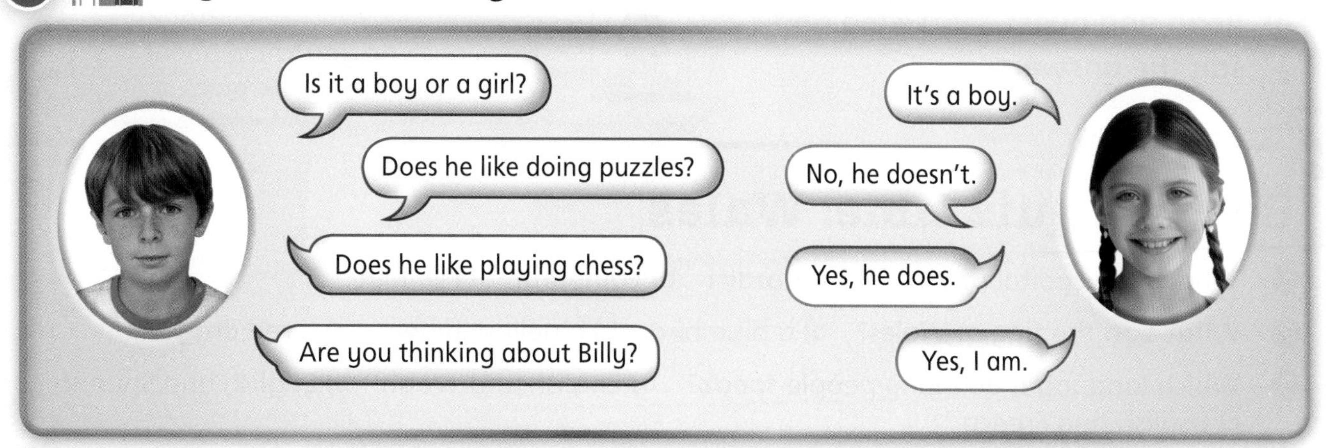

Is it a boy or a girl?
It's a boy.
Does he like doing puzzles?
No, he doesn't.
Does he like playing chess?
Yes, he does.
Are you thinking about Billy?
Yes, I am.

18 **Talk about you and your friends.**

I don't like playing computer games, but I love using the internet. My friend Paul likes taking photos.

FAST TRACK GRAMMAR *Write five sentences about what your friends like or don't like doing.*

Wales is a small country, but its culture is rich and varied. It has got its own language, Welsh, and strong traditions in music and sport. POST ✓

Lesson 6

19 CD1 19 **Listen and read.**

Welsh Culture

LANGUAGE

About 20% of Welsh people are bilingual. They speak English and Welsh. Welsh is a very old language, and people are making an effort to keep the language alive. At schools in Wales, all children have Welsh lessons. And most of the road signs in Wales are in both English and Welsh.

MUSIC

Wales is sometimes called 'the land of song'. Music is an important part of Welsh culture. Many pop stars and opera singers come from Wales, like Stereophonics, Tom Jones and Charlotte Church. But the country is especially famous for its male voice choirs. Many boys and men of all ages join choirs. They meet every week to practise. They sing songs in Welsh and in English.

SPORT

People in Wales play many kinds of sport, but the national sport is rugby. Rugby is a very physical sport. In rugby, you can score goals and tries. You score a goal when you kick the ball between the other team's goal posts. You score a try when you put the ball on the ground behind the other team's goal line. There are men's rugby teams and women's rugby teams, too.

What is your country famous for? Are people bilingual in your country?

20 **Read and guess.**

Listen and say the answers.

How much do you know about Wales? Do this culture quiz. POST ✓

Culture quiz time: Wales

1. What's the capital of Wales? a) Cardiff b) Edinburgh c) Dublin
2. What's on the flag of Wales? a) a blue bird b) a yellow flower c) a red dragon
3. Which languages do many people speak? a) English and Welsh b) English and Spanish c) English and French
4. Which famous writer is from Wales? a) J.K. Rowling b) Enid Blyton c) Roald Dahl
5. Who is the patron saint of Wales? a) St George b) St David c) St Andrew
6. Which vegetable is the national symbol of Wales? a) the leek b) the carrot c) the potato

In the UK there are many POST places to watch sports and pop concerts. Wembley Stadium is one of the most famous.

Lesson 7

Listen and read. Say *True* or *False*.

1 Wembley Stadium is in London.
2 It is bigger than all the other stadiums in Europe.
3 The stadium has a capacity of 90,000 people for a football match.
4 Every year, the final of the football World Cup is at Wembley Stadium.
5 Some football matches at the Olympic Games in 2012 were at Wembley Stadium.
6 Famous pop stars such as Shakira, Justin Beiber and One Direction sometimes give concerts in the stadium.

Everyday chit-chat

How to invite a friend to a concert

Listen and repeat.

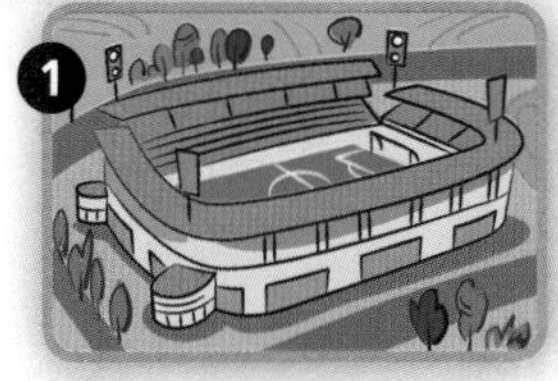

1 a stadium

2 a pop concert

3 a spare ticket

4 quarter past three

Listen and read. Repeat. 

Carrie: Hello?
Ed: Hi, Carrie. It's Ed.
Carrie: Hi. How are you?
Ed: I'm fine, thanks. I'm calling to see if you're free on Saturday night.
Carrie: Yes, I am. Why?
Ed: Well, my family has got tickets to see One Direction, at Wembley stadium.
Carrie: Wow! You're so lucky. One Direction is my favourite pop group.
Ed: Well, would you like to see the concert with us? My brother has got a bad cold, so we've got a spare ticket.
Carrie: Oh yes. Wow! I'd love to! Just let me ask my dad.

Carrie: Hi, Ed. My dad says I can go. I'm so excited!
Ed: Good. We can pick you up from your house at quarter past three on Saturday afternoon.
Carrie: OK. That's great. Thank you, Ed.

  **Do a role play.**

Lesson 8

Hi there! In Wales, lots of people are bilingual. I speak English at home. At school, I speak Welsh, and I'm learning French, too. Here's an article from our school magazine. Two people talk about the languages they're learning.

POST ✓

25 Listen and read.

Differences and similarities in languages

There are more than 6,000 different languages in the world. Some of these languages have similar vocabulary and grammar, but many are completely different.

For example:

- Some languages give nouns a gender. The nouns can be masculine, feminine or neutral. Other languages don't give nouns a gender.
- Some languages use the letters of an alphabet to write words. Other languages use characters instead of words.
- Some languages don't conjugate verbs. Other languages have many different conjugations.

the Japanese character for 'rain'

How do you say 'Do you live in Wales?' in Welsh?

Ydych chi'n byw yng Nghymru?

People learning foreign languages

Harry. I'm learning Japanese because my brother lives in Japan. Some aspects of Japanese are easy. For example, there aren't any verb conjugations, and nouns don't have a gender. But reading and writing in Japanese is very difficult for me. There are thousands of different characters to learn. And when you read a sentence, you don't read it from left to right. You read it from top to bottom.

Vanessa. I'm English, but I live in Wales. I'm learning Welsh because I want to speak to my Welsh friends in Welsh. In English, nouns don't have a gender, so it's difficult for me to remember the gender of nouns in Welsh. And spelling Welsh words isn't easy. But I love speaking the Welsh language, and I'm very happy with my progress.

THINKING SKILLS
Comparing and contrasting

26 Read and answer.

1. Which language is written in characters?
2. Which language doesn't conjugate verbs?
3. Which language gives nouns a gender?
4. Which language do you read in a different direction?
5. What things do Harry and Vanessa think are difficult about learning a language?

27 Play *Read and change.* Bridge to ESO

There are more than 6,000 different languages in Europe.

Stop! It doesn't say Europe. It says the world.

28 Think and say.

What do you like about learning English?

What do you think is easy and difficult?

My words to remember

letters of an alphabet characters gender conjugate verbs Japanese Welsh

INTERNET TRACKS Find out how to write the numbers 1 to 10 in Japanese characters.

Project: Free time survey

29 Look at the graph. Listen and read.

I asked 20 people at my school about the activities they like doing in their free time. Here are the results of my survey.

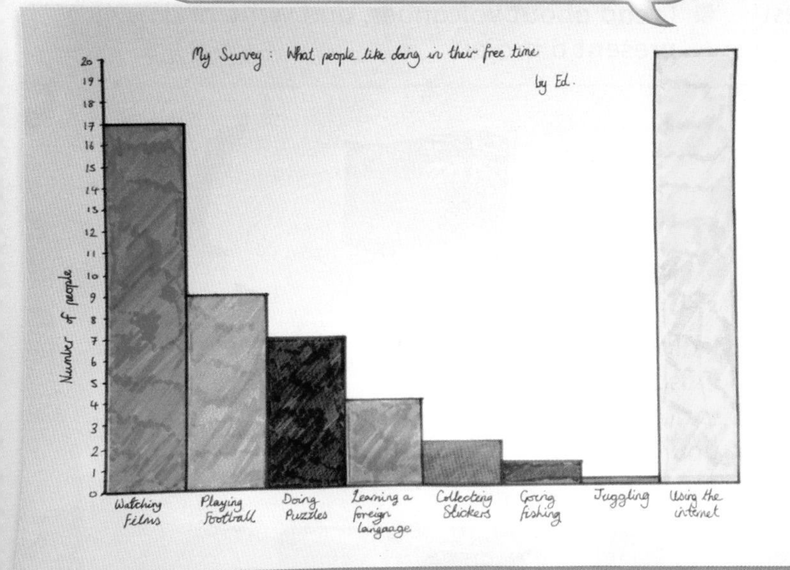

Yesterday, I presented this project in class. Which activities are very popular? Which activities are not popular? POST ✓

I wasn't surprised to find out that our favourite activities are using the internet and watching films. But I was very surprised to find out that nobody juggles in their free time. I love juggling. It's one of my favourite activities.

30 Plan your project.

1. Write questions.
2. Interview people.
3. Draw your results.
4. Write and present your results.

THINKING SKILLS
Analysing

You can also present your results using a pie chart.

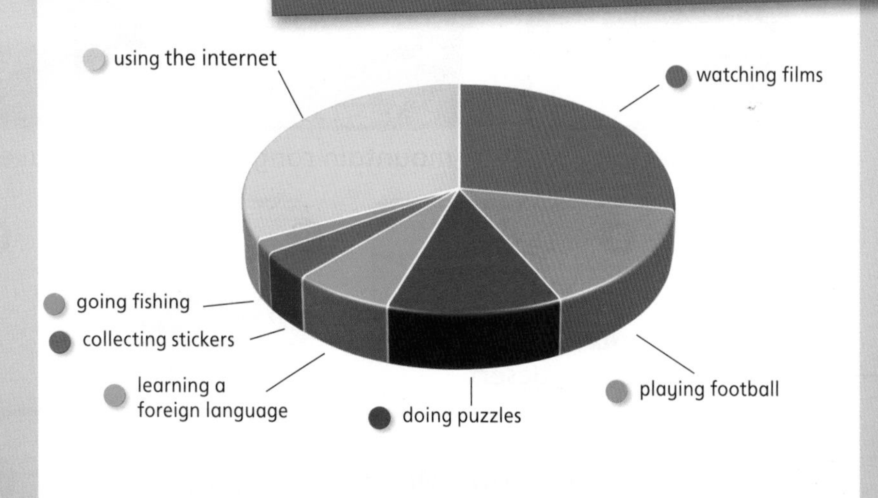

➔ AB page 12

Do the Unit 1 Review and self-assessment (Activity Book page 12). Complete your *Progress Journal* for Unit 1.

2 Geographical wonders

AIMS

In this unit:

- I **name** and **describe** geographical features.
- I **listen to** and **read** a biography *Sir Edmund Hillary.*
- I **talk about** the highest and longest geographical features.
- I **find out about** New Zealand and UK culture.
- I **act out** describing what I can see in a role play.
- I **read about** volcanoes, and **write** and **present** a project.

Lesson 1

Listen and say. 

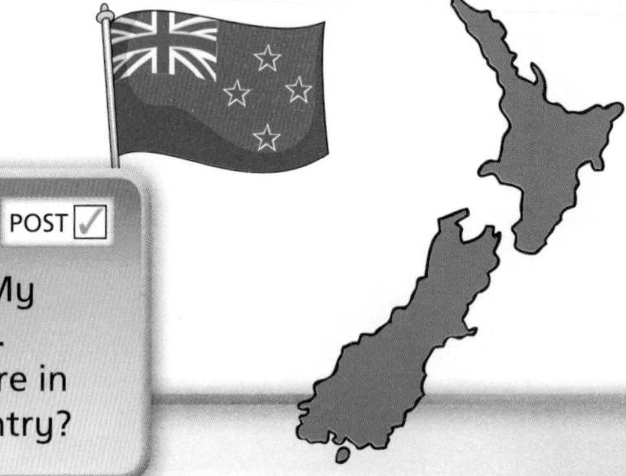

Tiger Tracks SLN POST

Hi. My name's Scott. I'm from New Zealand. My country is famous for its beautiful landscapes. Which of these geographical features are there in New Zealand? Can you see them in your country?

1 volcano

2 glacier

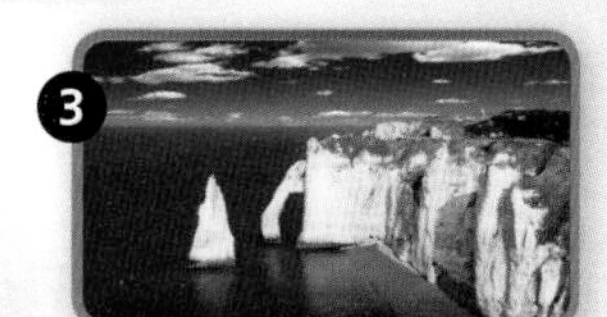

3 cliff

4 waterfall

5 mountain range

6 cave

7 rainforest

8 desert

9 island

10 valley

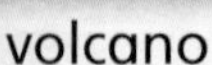

2 Listen and find out. Which geographical features are there in New Zealand?

 **Now ask and talk about your country.**

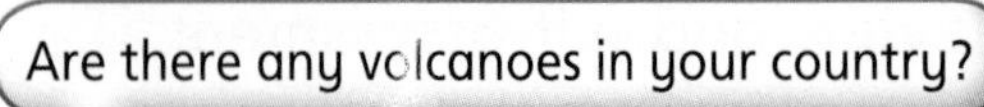
Are there any volcanoes in your country?

Yes, there are. I'm not sure. No, there aren't.

3 Listen and do the vocabulary quiz.

It's made of ice.
It moves very slowly.

INTERNET TRACKS Find out how far it is from New Zealand to Australia.

Lesson 2

4 Listen and read.

Here's a website about the POST incredible landscape of New Zealand! Which island do you think is more interesting to visit?

The natural beauty of New Zealand

READING TIP
Don't worry about the pronunciation of place names.

New Zealand is a country in the Southern Hemisphere. It has got two main islands. One is called North Island and the other is called South Island. There are many different areas of natural beauty to see on both islands.

North Island is 113,729 square kilometres. There are fantastic beaches on the west coast. There are rainforests where you can see rare plants and wildlife. There are mountains and there are lots of volcanoes. The largest volcano is called Mount Ruapehu. It is 2,797 metres high and it is an active volcano. New Zealand's largest lake is on North Island. It is called Lake Taupo. And one of the most popular tourist attractions is the Waitomo Caves.

Waterfall in the Whirinaki Rainforest

Westland National Park

South Island is 151,215 square kilometres. It is more mountainous than North Island. The Southern Alps is a mountain range that starts in the north of South Island and finishes in the south. Mount Cook is in the Southern Alps. It is 3,754 metres high, and it is the highest mountain in New Zealand. Fiordland is the country's largest national park. You can see mountains, glaciers, valleys and lakes in the park. It is very popular with climbers and hikers.

THINKING SKILLS
Comparing

5 Answer the questions.

1. Which is bigger, North Island or South Island?
2. Which island has got more mountains?
3. Where can you see New Zealand's largest lake?
4. What is the name of the largest national park?
5. What is the Southern Alps?

6 Play a memory game.

Where can you see caves?

On North Island!

7 Choose and say.

TALK ABOUT IT!

I want to visit New Zealand because I want to see the volcanoes.

INTERNET TRACKS Find out what insect lives in the Waitomo Caves.

Lesson 3 

8 Listen to and read the story.

This story is the biography of Sir Edmund Hillary, a famous climber from New Zealand. He lived from 1919 to 2008. His image is on the New Zealand $5 note. He is one of my favourite people from history. Enjoy! ☺ POST

Sir Edmund Hillary

- Why is Sir Edmund Hillary famous?
- Who saves his life in the story?

1 It is 1931. Edmund is eleven. On the train to school, he often reads adventure stories and books about explorers.

In the future, I want to be an explorer.

2 As a young man, Edmund climbs cliffs, mountains and volcanoes in New Zealand. He sometimes climbs with friends, but he often climbs alone.

3 It is 1953. Edmund is 33. He goes to Nepal to climb Mount Everest, the highest mountain in the world.

Kathmandu

4 In the expedition to climb Mount Everest, there are 11 climbers, a journalist, a photographer, a doctor, and 350 porters to carry all the food and equipment. Edmund talks to Tenzing Norgay, a climber from Nepal.

Hello, Tenzing.

9 **Read and answer the questions.**

1. What types of books does Edmund read as a boy?
2. When does Edmund go to Nepal?
3. How many porters are on the expedition to climb Everest?
4. Edmund nearly dies during the expedition. How?
5. How high is Mount Everest?
6. How long do Edmund and Tenzing stand on top of Everest?

Is it sometimes important to work as a team? Why?
When do you work in a team?

5 The climbers begin their ascent. Edmund climbs with Tenzing. A rope connects them. It's extremely cold. And very windy.

6 During the expedition, Edmund falls through a crack in the ice. Tenzing reacts quickly and saves Edmund's life.

Don't worry! You are safe.
Thank you, my friend!

7 The climbers climb for six long weeks. At 7,900 metres the temperature is extremely cold. The oxygen is thin. Some of the climbers can't feel their feet. Some of them feel sick.

We can't reach the top. We cannot continue.
Tenzing, we can reach the top. I know we can do it.

8 At 8,800 metres, Edmund and Tenzing are alone. They haven't got much oxygen. And the last 50 metres are the most dangerous.

9 On 29th May at 11:30am, Edmund and Tenzing are the first climbers in history to reach the top of Mount Everest. They are at 8,850 metres. They stand there for 15 minutes and look at the view. Edmund takes photos.

We did it, my friend! We did it!

It is one of the most important moments in the history of climbing.

Do you know...?

After Tenzing Norgay and Edmund Hillary climbed Everest, journalists asked 'Who reached the top first?' They answered, 'We reached the top together, as a team.'

10 Ask and say.

1 Do you like the story? Why? / Why not?
2 What's your favourite part of the story?
3 Does anything in the story surprise you?
4 Do you want to climb Mount Everest?

Everyday phrases: learn and use!

It's good to see you.
It's extremely cold.
It's very windy.
We did it!

Lesson 4

11 Listen and read. Answer the questions in the first paragraph.

Guinness World Records – a reference book

Which is **the highest** mountain in the world? Which is **the widest** river in the world? Which is **the smelliest** frog in the world? Which is **the most dangerous** shark in the world? When you ask questions like these, where do you find the answers? Do you look for the answers on the internet, or in an encyclopaedia? Or do you look in a book called *Guinness World Records*?

Guinness World Records is a reference book. It contains information about **the highest, the smelliest, the hottest, the longest** and **the most exceptional** things in the world. For example, Mount Everest is **the highest** mountain in the world, the Sahara is **the hottest** desert, the Amazon is **the widest** river, and the Pacific is **the deepest** ocean.

The smelliest frog is the venezuelan skunk frog. And **the most dangerous** shark in the world is the great white shark.

There are also *Guinness World Records* museums and a *Guinness World Records* website.

12 Work in groups. Play *Team Reading Race*.

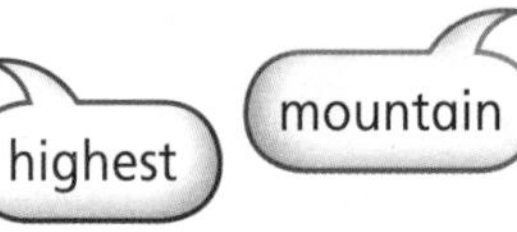

13 Listen, repeat and learn.

Superlative adjectives

I'm	tall.
You're	young.
He's	noisy.
She's	big.
It's	strange.
We're	intelligent.
They're	interesting.

I'm	the tallest			
You're	the youngest	person		
He's	the noisiest	place		the world.
She's	the biggest	animal	in	our class.
It's	the strangest			my family.
We're	the most intelligent	people		
They're	the most interesting	animals		

14 Be a grammar detective! Look at page 17 in the AB.

When do we use superlative adjectives?

How do we make superlative adjectives?

How many superlative adjectives can you find in the story?

FAST TRACK GRAMMAR *Write five sentences about your family using superlative adjectives.*

Lesson 5

15 Listen and read. Identify two ways to pronounce *-est*.

This bird's n**est** isn't the cheap**est**, but it's the b**est**. It's the bigg**est** and the strong**est** and it's a lovely place to r**est**.

16 Look. Listen and answer the questions.

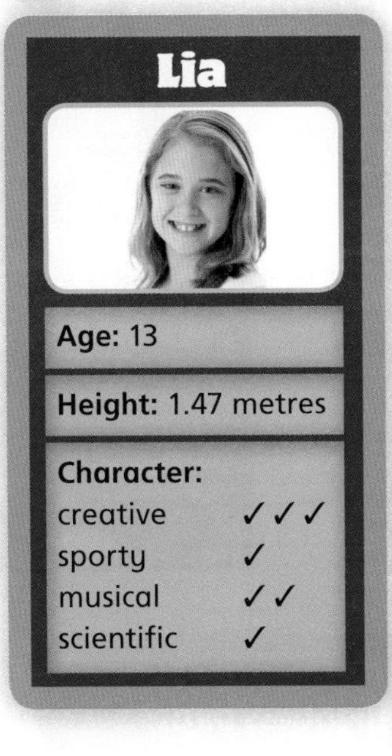

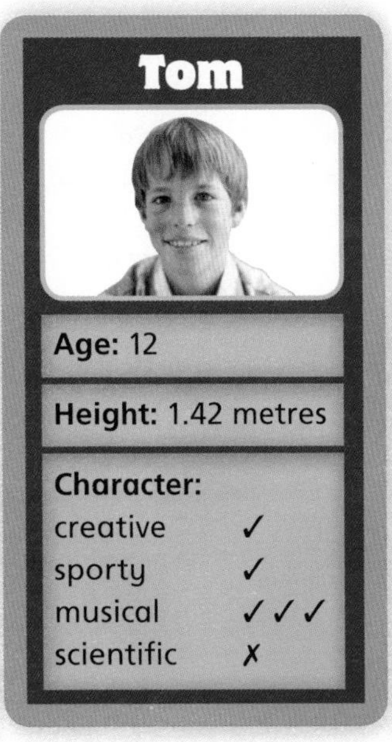

17 Play *Who am I?*

Are you the youngest?
No, I'm not.
Are you the most musical?
No, I'm not.
Are you the sportiest?
Yes, I am.
You're Jane!
Yes, that's right.

18 Talk about you and your friends.

John is the youngest. Lisa is the most scientific.
Laura hasn't got the longest hair.

FAST TRACK GRAMMAR *Write five superlative sentences about the people in your class.*

POST ✓

The kiwi is a bird that lives in New Zealand. It is a symbol of my country. Many other birds also live in New Zealand. In fact, the country is sometimes called 'the land of birds'.

Cult

Lesson 6

19  **Listen and read.**

New Zealand, the Land of Birds

There are many animals in New Zealand that you cannot see anywhere else in the world. There are very rare types of spider, dolphin, lizard and sea lion. But New Zealand is most famous for its birds. Many of these birds are unique to New Zealand because they are flightless birds. They cannot fly, so they cannot travel to other countries.

1 **The kakapo** is a type of parrot. It is the only flightless parrot in the world. The adults can weigh over three kilograms, so the kakapo is also the heaviest species of parrot in the world.

2 **The blue penguin** lives in many parts of New Zealand. There are 17 species of penguin in the world, and many of them live in New Zealand. The blue penguin has got blue-grey feathers and it is the smallest species of penguin. It is about 30 cm long and it weighs about one kilogram.

3 **The kiwi** is a flightless bird with a very long beak. A kiwi is about the same size as a chicken. But a kiwi's egg is six times larger than a chicken's egg! The male kiwi incubates the egg and looks after it for about 80 days. 80 days! That's the longest incubation period of any bird in the world.

What species of birds live in your country? Are any of them flightless birds?

20 Read and guess. CD1 41 **Listen and say the answers.**

POST ✓

Now it's my turn to give you a culture quiz on New Zealand. Are you ready?

Culture quiz time: New Zealand

1. What's the capital of New Zealand? **a)** Queensland **b)** Wellington **c)** Auckland
2. Who are the indigenous people of New Zealand? **a)** the Maoris **b)** the Aborigines **c)** the Inuits
3. What are the official languages of New Zealand? **a)** Maori and English **b)** English and French **c)** Maori and Spanish
4. What's the population of New Zealand? **a)** 4 million **b)** 14 million **c)** 24 million
5. What is New Zealand money called? **a)** euros **b)** dollars **c)** pounds
6. What are people from New Zealand sometimes called? **a)** penguins **b)** parrots **c)** kiwis

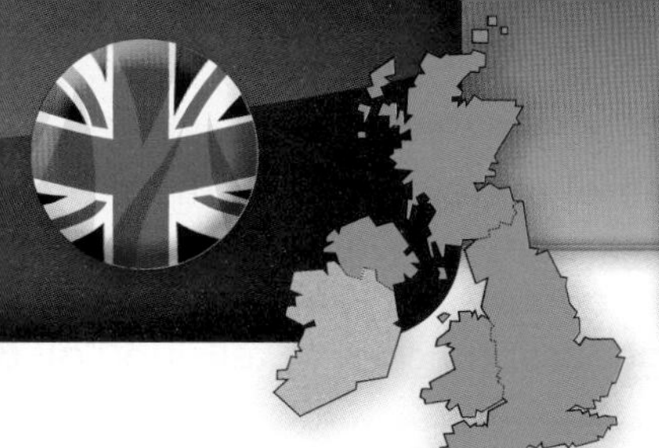

POST ✓

We've got some interesting birds in the UK. And bird watching is a popular activity.

Lesson 7

Listen and read. Say *True* or *False*.

1 There are more than 1,000 different bird species in the UK.
2 The RSPB is an organisation that protects birds in the UK.
3 Many families in the UK feed wild birds in their living rooms.
4 Some families have got bird boxes in their gardens.
5 The robin is one of the most common birds in UK gardens.
6 Collecting birds' eggs is a crime in the UK.

Everyday chit-chat

How to describe what you can see

Listen and repeat.

1 binoculars

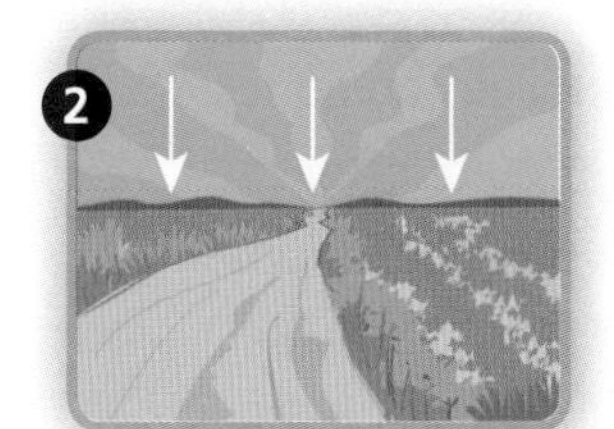

2 horizon

3 hills

4 building

Listen and read. Repeat.

Ed: Look. The view from up here is great.
Carrie: Yes, it is. What's that big white building over there?
Ed: That's the hospital. And on the right of it, you can see my school.
Carrie: Oh yes. And what's that over there, on the horizon?
Ed: Those are the hills where we went yesterday and had a picnic.
Carrie: Can I have the binoculars for a moment?
Ed: Of course. What can you see?
Carrie: Not a lot.
Ed: Because you've got the binoculars the wrong way round!
Carrie: Oh yeah! You're right! Ah, that's better!

Do a role play.

Hi there! In New Zealand there are lots of volcanoes. At school, we learn about volcanoes in our geography lessons. This text is a project from my geography class. It tells you all about volcanoes. POST

Lesson 8

25 Listen and read.

Volcanoes

What is a volcano?

Inside the earth, there is a layer of very hot liquid rock. A volcano is a place where this hot rock can escape through a hole in the surface. When this happens, we call it a volcanic eruption. When a volcano erupts, the hot liquid rock cools down in the air and solidifies on the surface around the hole. Because of this, most volcanoes are mountains.

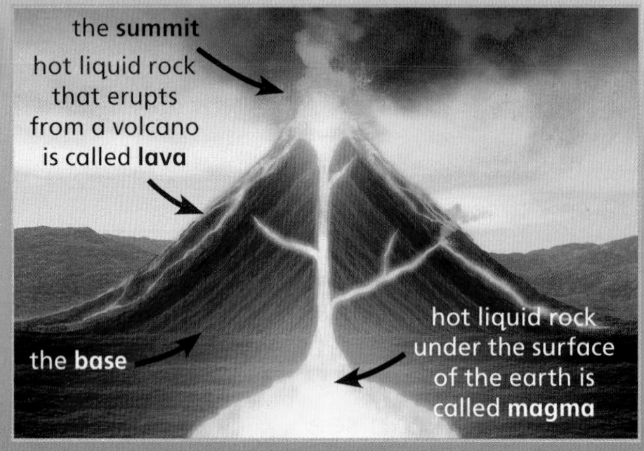

Types of volcano

We can put volcanoes in three categories:

1. **Active volcanoes** erupt quite often.
2. **Dormant** or **inactive volcanoes** erupted a long time ago, but they can erupt again.
3. **Extinct volcanoes** cannot erupt again.

The tallest volcano

The tallest volcano in the world is a dormant volcano called Mauna Kea. It is on the island of Hawaii. The base of Mauna Kea is 6,000 metres below sea level. The summit is 4,205 metres above sea level. From the base to the summit, Mauna Kea is 10,205 metres tall.

The largest volcano in the solar system

The largest volcano in the solar system is on Mars. It is called Olympus Mons. It is an incredible 25 kilometres high! That's three times higher than Mount Everest!

THINKING SKILLS
Defining

27 Play *Volcanic words.*

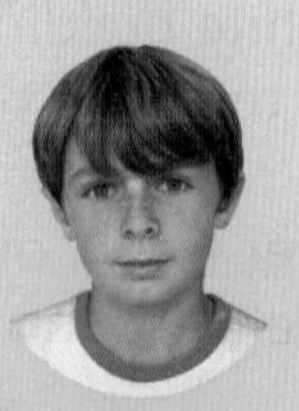

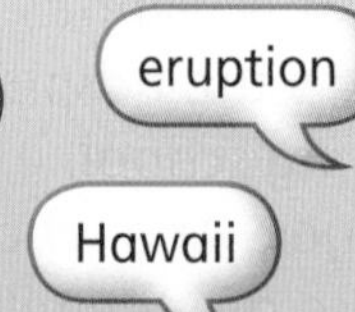

26 Read and define. Bridge to ESO

Define these words:

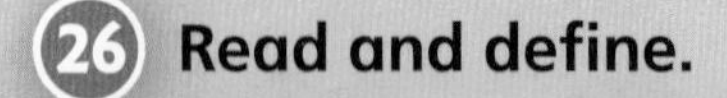
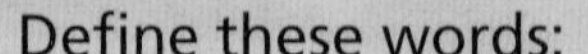

1 volcano
2 magma
3 lava
4 volcanic eruption

28 Think and say.

Are there any volcanoes in your country or in a country near you?

What types of volcano are they?

My words to remember

base summit volcanic rock lava eruption magma

INTERNET TRACKS Find out the name of the most active volcano in the world.

Project: Superlative quiz

29 CD2 **Listen and read.**

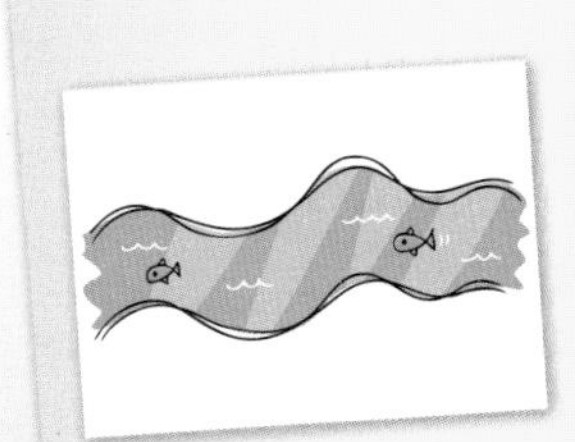

What's the widest river in the world?
a) the Amazon
b) the Nile
c) the Thames

What's the most populated country in the world?
a) India
b) the UK
c) China

Yesterday at school, I made these superlative quiz cards. Can you answer the questions? POST

Becky: Question number 1. What's the widest river in the world? Is it a) the Amazon, b) the Nile or c) the Thames?

Friend: I think the answer is the Nile.

Becky: I'm sorry. It isn't the Nile. The widest river in the world is the Amazon. The Nile is the longest.

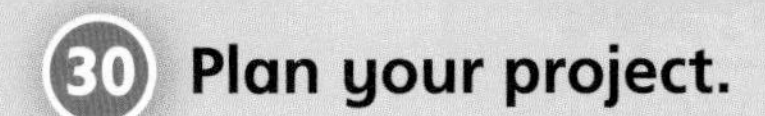

30 **Plan your project.**

THINKING SKILLS
Remembering

You can also present your quiz on a computer.

1. Find out superlative facts about animals and geographical features.
2. Prepare your questions.
3. Think of two incorrect answers for each question.
4. Write and present your quiz.

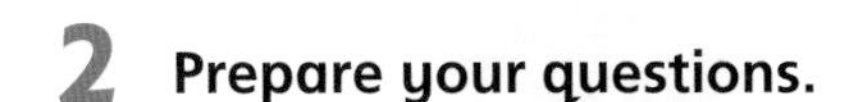

Which is the smallest type of penguin in the world?

A. the blue penguin

B. the emperor penguin

C. the king penguin

AB page 22

Do the Unit 2 Review and Self-assessment (Activity Book page 22). Complete your *Progress Journal* for Unit 2.

3 Recipes and food

In this unit:

- I **name** and **describe** different types of food.
- I **listen to** and **read** a survival story *The hurricane and the coconut tree.*
- I **ask** and **answer** questions about food.
- I **find out about** Jamaican and UK culture.
- I **act out** giving instructions in the kitchen in a role play.
- I **read about** products from trees, and **write** and **present** a project.

Lesson 1

1 CD2 6 **Listen and say.** 

Tiger Tracks SLN POST

Hi there. I'm Florence from Jamaica. We have lots of kinds of food in my country. Which of these foods does Jamaica produce? Does your country produce the same foods?

1 coconuts

2 salt

3 coffee

4 spices

5 beans

6 citrus fruits

7 rice

8 honey

9 sugar

10 olives

2 CD2 7 **Listen and find out. Which foods does Jamaica produce?** **Now ask and talk about your country.**

Does your country produce coffee?

Yes, I think so. | I'm not really sure. | No, I don't think so.

3 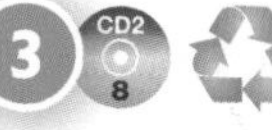  CD2 8 **Listen and do the vocabulary quiz.**

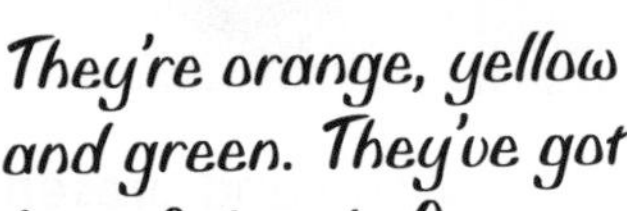

They're orange, yellow and green. They've got lots of vitamin C.

INTERNET TRACKS Find a map of Jamaica. What is the name of the capital city? Where is it?

Lesson 2

4 **Listen and read.**

I love learning about food and cooking. POST
This is one of my favourite food blogs. I always find interesting information here, and simple but tasty recipes too! Do you think this cake looks good?

Jamaican coconuts

Use a dictionary to find out the meaning of new words if they are important, e.g. *teaspoon* and *grated*.

Jamaica is a Caribbean island. Coconut trees grow very well in the country's warm, tropical climate. There are many coconut farms on the island and coconut is a popular ingredient in Jamaican cooking.

Jamaican Coconut Cake

Today's recipe is a cake full of Jamaican flavours. There's some coconut in it, but there are also two more ingredients from Jamaica: chocolate and lime. The cake is delicious and very simple to make.

Ingredients

175g of butter
100g of brown sugar
1 tablespoon of honey
3 eggs
175g of flour, with 2 teaspoons of baking powder
¼ of a teaspoon of salt
50g of coconut
The juice of a lime
50g of grated dark chocolate

Instructions

1. First of all, put the butter, sugar and honey into a bowl. Mix until the mixture is smooth.
2. Then, add the eggs one at a time. Mix after each egg.
3. Slowly add the flour, coconut and grated chocolate and mix well. Then add the lime juice and mix again.
4. Next, pour the mixture into a greased baking tin.
5. Last of all, put it in the oven and bake it for 30–35 minutes at 180°. Leave the cake to cool.

Serving Suggestion

Serve the cake with a glass of lemonade. Enjoy!

THINKING SKILLS
Explaining and sequencing

5 **Answer the questions.**

1. What type of climate has Jamaica got?
2. Which three ingredients from Jamaica are in the cake?
3. How many teaspoons of salt do you need?
4. How long do you bake the cake for?
5. What drink is good with the cake?

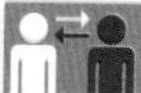

6 **Play *Read and change*.**

Jamaica is a Caribbean city.

Stop! It doesn't say city. It says island.

7 **Think and say.** TALK ABOUT IT!

I think Jamaican Coconut Cake looks delicious. I want to try it.

INTERNET TRACKS Find out the names of three more countries in the Caribbean.

Lesson 3

8 Listen to and read the story.

Sometimes there are hurricanes in Jamaica. Our grandparents all remember very bad hurricanes. They've all got a survival story to tell us. This is one story. I hope you like it.

THE HURRICANE AND THE COCONUT TREE

- How strong is the hurricane?
- How old is the coconut tree?

1 Zach and his mother are on holiday in Jamaica. They are visiting their friends Alice and Jake.

Look, Mum! There are coconuts in the tree.
And there's milk inside each coconut.

Zach, let me tell you a story about this tree.

2 One day, in Jamaica, there's an important message on the radio.

Hurricane Gilbert is moving towards the island of Jamaica. It is a force five hurricane.

3 Everybody on the island prepares for the hurricane. They protect their houses and their animals. They put extra food and drink in their cupboards.

Are there any bottles of water? Is there any bread?
Yes, don't worry. There are five bottles of water and there's some bread. We've got everything we need.

4 Later, the sky is very cloudy. The wind is very strong. The hurricane is near.

I don't believe it! Look! There's a girl with a tent under the coconut tree.

9 Read and say *True* or *False*. Correct the false sentences.

1. Zach and his mum live in Jamaica.
2. People hear about the hurricane on the radio.
3. Alice and Jake see a girl in a car under the coconut tree.
4. The girl in the story is Zach's sister.
5. Zach's mum saved Alice and Jake's life.
6. In picture 9, the coconut tree is more than 20 years old.

Is it important to prepare for the weather? Why?

How do you prepare for the weather in your country?

5

6

When the eye of the hurricane travels across the island, it destroys everything in its path. It picks up the coconut tree and drops it on top of the girl's tent.

7

The day after the storm, there aren't many trees standing. The girl feels very lucky to be alive.

8

The girl in the story was your mother, more than 25 years ago.
I was very silly to put my tent under a tree. Jake and Alice saved my life. And a week after the hurricane, I planted this coconut tree to say thank you and to help repair the land.

Do you know...?

We give hurricanes names. Hurricane Gilbert devastated Jamaica in 1988. It destroyed towns, farms and the countryside. Sadly, it also killed 200 people.

9

Good catch!
I think the tree likes you, Zach. It's giving you a coconut!
Can I try some coconut milk now, please?

10 Ask and say.

1. Do you like the story? Why? / Why not?
2. What's your favourite part of the story?
3. Do you think it was a good idea to plant a tree to say thank you to Jake and Alice?
4. Do you want to visit Jamaica?

Everyday phrases: learn and use!

Try some. It's delicious!

The wind is very strong.

I don't believe it!

A hurricane is coming. It isn't safe to stay here under this tree.
Please, come inside with us.

GRAMMAR TRACKS

Lesson 4

11 Listen and read. Predict what they want to make.

Father: **Is there any** flour in the cupboard?
Boy: Yes, there is. **There are two** packets of flour. And **there are three** boxes of sugar.
Father: **Is there any** milk in the fridge?
Girl: Yes, there is. **There are four** bottles of milk. And **there's some** butter, too.
Father: **Are there any** eggs?
Boy: Yes, there are.
Girl: **There are three,** four, five eggs.
Father: OK. We've got all the ingredients we need. Let's make …

12 Act out the dialogue.

13 Listen, repeat and learn. 

Countable and uncountable nouns

There	is	an egg.
	are	some eggs.

There	isn't	a bottle of milk.
	aren't	any bottles of milk.

Is	there	an apple?	Yes,	there is.	No,	there isn't.
Are		any apples?		there are.		there aren't.

Uncountable nouns

There	is	some milk.

There	isn't	any flour.

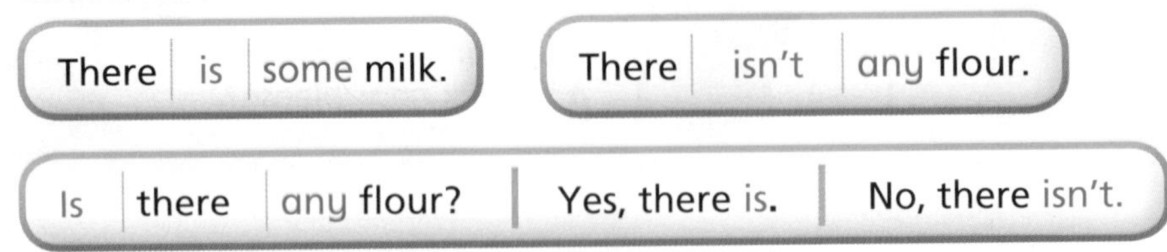

Is	there	any flour?	Yes, there is.	No, there isn't.

14 Be a grammar detective! Look at page 27 in the AB.

Can you count flour?
Can you count packets of flour?
Do we use *There is…* or *There are…* with uncountable nouns?

Can you find five examples of these structures in the story?
There is(n't) + uncountable noun
There are(n't) + countable noun

FAST TRACK GRAMMAR *Write a list of uncountable nouns that are in your school.*

Lesson 5

15 **Listen and read. What do you notice about the words in green? Listen and repeat.**

Look! There are two chickens sitting on their legs.
They're not sitting on their legs, they're sitting on their eggs.

16 CD2 15 **Listen and say *True* or *False*. Correct the false sentences.**

17 **Play *Which cupboard?***

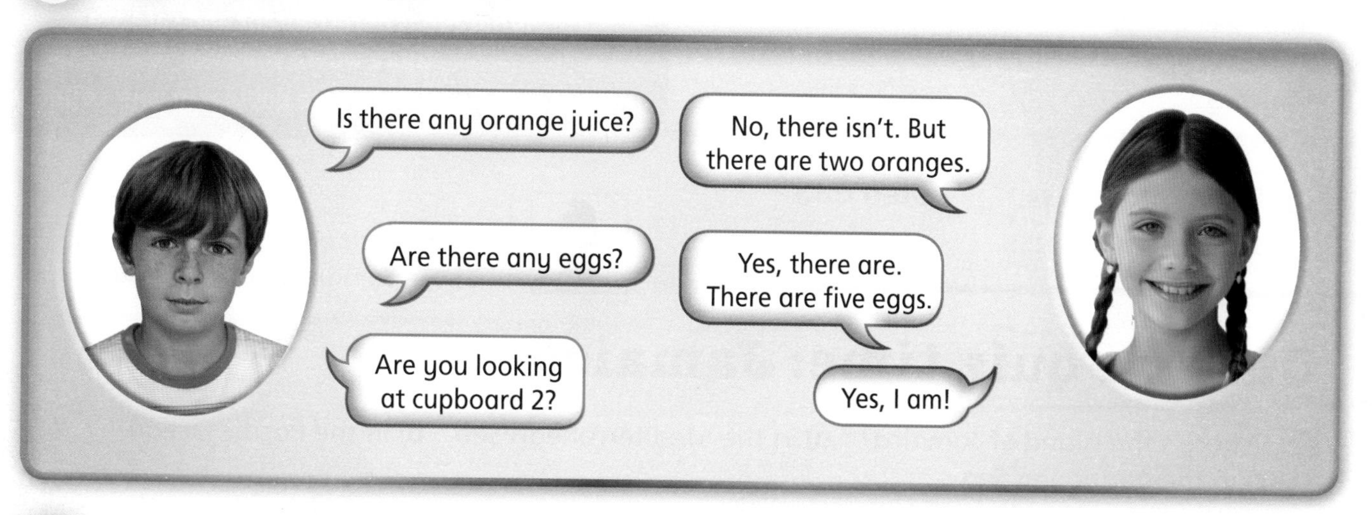

Is there any orange juice?
No, there isn't. But there are two oranges.
Are there any eggs?
Yes, there are. There are five eggs.
Are you looking at cupboard 2?
Yes, I am!

18 **Write a list of five foods in your fridge. Ask and answer questions.**

Have you got any milk in your fridge?

Yes, I have. I've got some cheese.

No, I haven't. Have you got any cheese in your fridge?

FAST TRACK GRAMMAR *Write a dialogue like the one in Activity 17 using different foods.*

In Jamaica, you can eat lots of different kinds of international food. This article makes me want to try dishes from different countries around the world.

POST ✓

Lesson 6

19 Listen and read.

Eating out in Kingston, Jamaica

In Kingston, the capital of Jamaica, there are many different types of restaurant and café. They cook food from lots of different countries around the world. There are Spanish bars where you can try tapas and paella. There are Italian pizzerias where you can try different types of pasta and pizza. There are Japanese restaurants where you can try sushi. Or how about a curry at an Indian restaurant? Or a chilli con carne at a Mexican restaurant? They're all delicious. But if you're on holiday in Jamaica, why not try a traditional Jamaican dish? Jamaican cooking includes lots of the ingredients that the island produces. It is often fruity and spicy.

pizza

sushi

curry

Jamaican rice with red beans
This very popular dish is made with rice, coconut milk, onions, spices and red beans. It's delicious. Jamaicans often have it with chicken for lunch on Sunday.

Baked Jamaican bananas
In Jamaica you can eat red bananas! They are smaller and sweeter than yellow bananas. You can bake them with butter, sugar, lime juice and spices. People eat them hot with ice cream. Mmm. Delicious.

Lemonade
This cool, refreshing drink is very popular all year in Jamaica. It's made with lemons, limes, water, brown sugar and spices. A glass of lemonade with ice really is the taste of Jamaica!

What types of restaurant and café are there where you live?
What traditional dishes are popular in your country?

20 Read and guess. Listen and say the answers.

How much do you know about Jamaica? Let's find out.

POST ✓

Culture quiz time: Jamaica

1. Where's the island of Jamaica? **a)** in the Mediterranean Sea **b)** in the Pacific Ocean **c)** in the Caribbean Sea
2. What's the capital of Jamaica? **a)** Kingston **b)** Queenston **c)** Princeton
3. What's the official language of Jamaica? **a)** French **b)** English **c)** Spanish
4. What type of music comes from Jamaica? **a)** jazz **b)** reggae **c)** pop
5. What foods does Jamaica produce? **a)** bananas, sugar and spices **b)** olives, pumpkins and tea **c)** milk, cheese and yoghurt
6. In which sport does Jamaica have a lot of world champions? **a)** swimming **b)** football **c)** athletics

The UK is famous for fish and chips, and for roast beef. It is also famous for a traditional cooked breakfast.

POST ✓

Lesson 7

21 CD2 19 **Listen and read. Say *True* or *False*.**

1 A traditional cooked breakfast includes eggs, sausages, tomatoes, mushrooms, baked beans, toast and a large cup of tea or coffee.

2 In the past, it was the breakfast of farmers and workmen who needed lots of energy.

3 Nowadays, most people have lemon juice, cereal and toast for breakfast.

4 People never have a traditional British breakfast at the weekend.

5 "Brunch" is a combination of the words "breakfast" and "lunch".

Everyday chit-chat

! How to give instructions in the kitchen

22 CD2 20 **Listen and repeat.**

1 slice of bread

2 cream cheese

3 slices of apple

4 crisps

23 CD2 21 **Listen and read. Repeat.**

Ed: This is my favourite type of sandwich.
Carrie: What's in it?
Ed: Cream cheese, apple and crisps.
Carrie: That's unusual! How do you make it?
Ed: It's really easy. First, you put some cream cheese on a slice of bread. Then you put some slices of apple on the cheese.
Carrie: Then what?
Ed: Then you put some crisps on top of the apple.
Carrie: OK. That isn't difficult. What next?
Ed: Next, you put some more apple on top of the crisps. Last of all, you put another slice of bread on top of the apple and you press it down. Then you cut the sandwich in half and eat it.
Carrie: Mmmm! I don't believe it! It's delicious!

24 **Do a role play.**

Lesson 8

Hi there! I love trees. They give us coconuts, bananas and spices. But there are many other things that come from trees, too. Here's a website which tells us about some of the products we get from trees.

25 CD2 22 **Listen and read.**

Generous trees

Trees give us so many things. They give us fruit, chocolate and coconuts to eat and coffee to drink. They give us wood to make houses and furniture. And did you know that natural rubber comes from a tree too? Here are some more things that come from trees.

Oxygen
There is one thing that all trees give us. You can't see it, but it's all around us. It's in the air. It's oxygen. In a process called photosynthesis, trees absorb carbon dioxide and turn it into oxygen.

Medicines
Many types of medicine come from trees. Aspirin, for example. Aspirin is a natural product that comes from the bark of willow trees. In the 18th century, people used willow bark to make a type of tea. The tea helped people who were in pain. Nowadays, aspirin is made in laboratories.

Cork
Have you got a cork noticeboard at school? Where does the cork come from? It comes from the bark of a special type of oak tree. The tree grows in Spain, Portugal and France. People take the bark off the trees. This process does not harm the tree. The bark grows back every 7 to 10 years.

Paper
The main ingredient of paper is wood fibres. Factories mix wood fibres with water and chemicals to make paper. But factories can also make new paper from old magazines and newspapers. It's important to recycle paper because it saves trees.

Chewing gum
Natural chewing gum is made from a thick liquid that comes from the sapodilla tree. People cut the tree and collect the liquid in buckets. To make natural chewing gum, they add flavouring and sugar to the liquid.

THINKING SKILLS
Deciding and justifying

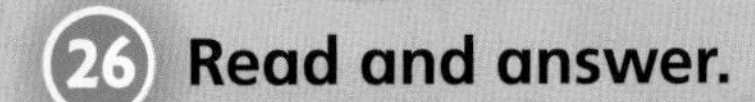

26 **Read and answer.**

1 Write a list of twelve things which come from trees.
2 In your opinion, which three things on your list are the most important? Why?

27 **Play *Search and find*. Write.**

Find in the text:
- *two things you can read*
- *three parts of a tree*
- *two types of gas*
- *three countries*
- *five things you can eat*
- *two things you can drink*

28 **Think and say.**

How many trees can you name in English?

What kinds of trees are near where you live?

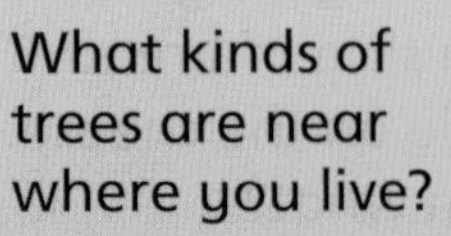

My words to remember
medicines cork
oxygen chewing gum
paper natural rubber

INTERNET TRACKS General Sherman is a tree in the USA. Find out why it is special.

Project: A recipe

This is my favourite recipe. It's easy and delicious. Have you got all the ingredients? Do you want to make it? POST ✓

Listen and read.

Baked apples with ice cream

Introduction

We've got an apple tree in our garden so we eat lots of apples. Baked apples with ice cream is one of my favourite desserts and it's very easy to make.

Ingredients

4 apples the same size
2 tablespoons of sultanas
1 teaspoon of cinnamon
4 teaspoons of butter
2 teaspoons of brown sugar

Preparation time

15 minutes

Cooking time

25 minutes

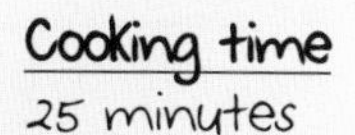

Instructions

- First of all, put the sultanas, the brown sugar and the cinnamon in a bowl and mix them together.
- Then, wash the apples. Cut out the centre of each apple. (Be very careful. Don't cut yourself. Ask someone to help you.)
- Next, put the apples in a dish. Put the sultanas, cinnamon and sugar mixture into each apple. And put a teaspoon of butter on top.
- Last of all, put the dish into the oven. Bake the apples at 200° for 20 to 25 minutes.

Serving suggestions

Serve your baked apples in a bowl with ice cream.

By Ed

30 Plan your project.

THINKING SKILLS
Explaining and sequencing

1 Choose a favourite dish.

2 Find out what ingredients you need.

3 Find out how to make the dish.

4 Write and present your recipe.

You can also present your project in this way.

First of all, put the sultanas, the brown sugar and the cinnamon in a bowl and mix them together.

AB page 32

Do the Unit 3 Review and self-assessment (Activity Book page 32). Complete your *Progress Journal* for Unit 3.

4 Around the city

In this unit:

- I **name** and **describe** places in towns and cities.
- I **listen to** and **read** a detective story *The alibi*.
- I **talk about** where people were at different times yesterday.
- I **find out about** Irish and UK culture.
- I **act out** finding out about opening and closing times in a role play.
- I **read about** how people use technology, and **write** and **present** a project.

Lesson 1

1 Listen and say. 

Tiger Tracks SLN POST

Hi everyone. My name's Finn. I live in Dublin, the capital of Ireland. I think it's a great city. Can you guess which of these things Dublin hasn't got? Have you got all these things where you live?

1 airport
2 botanical garden

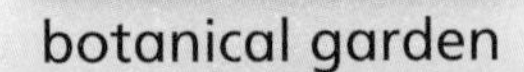

3 sports stadium

4 post office

5 port

6 bank

7 theme park

8 shopping centre

9 main square

10 tourist information office

2 **Listen and find out. Which places hasn't Dublin got? Now ask and talk about your town.**

Has your town got an airport?

Yes, it has. | I think so. | I don't think so. | No, it hasn't.

3 **Listen and do the vocabulary quiz.**

It's a place where you can see ships and boats.

INTERNET TRACKS Find a map of Ireland. What is the name of the capital city? Where is it?

Lesson 2

4 Listen and read.

At the moment, a girl from Spain is staying with my family. She's learning English. Yesterday, I helped her write this letter to her friends at home. Do you think Dublin is a good city to visit? POST ✓

Dear all,

This letter is in English because I need to practise writing. Finn is helping me.

I'm having lots of fun in Dublin. It's a great city! 😊😊 The people are friendly and my host family is fantastic, especially Finn. They've got a very nice house in the city centre. I can see Dublin Castle from my bedroom window. 😊

From Monday to Friday I go to school with Finn and his sister. The school isn't in the city centre. It takes twenty minutes to go by bus, but there's lots to see on the journey. Dublin is so beautiful! There are parks and museums. There are some incredible bridges over the river. There's a port. And, of course, there are lots of shopping centres. Fantastic! I love shopping! 😊😊

Last Saturday, I was at the sports stadium for a pop concert. The music wasn't very good ☹ but the stadium was amazing! 😊

My favourite place in Dublin is the botanical garden. Wow! It's gorgeous! I love looking at all the exotic plants.

See you soon.

Best wishes,

Ana

P.S. I hope you like the photos.

READING TIP The use of smiley faces can help you understand how the writer feels.

THINKING SKILLS
Reporting

5 Correct the sentences.

1. Ana says Dublin is a horrible city.
2. Ana says she can see a park from her window.
3. Ana says she hates shopping.
4. Ana says her favourite place is the stadium.
5. Ana says she loves looking at exotic animals.

6 Play *Read and change.*

Bridge to ESO

Dear everyone.

Stop. It doesn't say everyone. It says all.

7 Think and say.

TALK ABOUT IT!

I want to stay with a family in Dublin because I like people from Ireland.

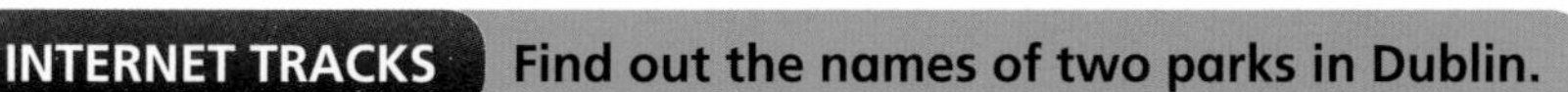

INTERNET TRACKS Find out the names of two parks in Dublin.

Lesson 3

8 Listen to and read the story.

POST ✓

In my free time, I like writing and illustrating stories. This is one of my detective stories. I hope you enjoy it.

The alibi

- Where does the robbery happen?
- How many people plan it?

1 Inspector Smith is from London, but today he's at the airport in Dublin.

14:05

It's five past two. My plane was on time. It's a sunny day. This is the perfect start to my holiday.

DUBLIN AIRPORT

2 Suddenly, a woman bumps into the Inspector. He falls to the ground.

DUBLIN AIRPORT

Oh no! Oh dear! Are you OK?

Yes, I think so.

My name's Olivia Jones and I'm not usually so clumsy.

Please don't worry, Miss Jones. I'm fine.

Wait, Miss Jones. Your earring!

3 The next day, Inspector Smith is reading his newspaper in the botanical garden.

DUBLINEWS

WOMAN STEALS DIAMOND FROM DUBLIN MUSEUM

At two o'clock yesterday afternoon, the biggest diamond in Ireland was in the museum. Ten minutes later, the diamond was missing. Police arrested Miss Olivia Jones. Witnesses say she was at the museum between 1:55 and 2:10

But that isn't possible. Miss Jones was at the airport at five past two.

4 At the police station …

DUBLIN POLICE STATION

11:40

Officer, I'm afraid this is a case of mistaken identity. This woman has got an alibi. She was with me at the time of the robbery.

9 Read and answer the questions.

1. Where is the inspector from?
2. Who is the woman at the airport?
3. When did the robbery happen?
4. What is special about the diamond?
5. Where do the police find the diamond?
6. How does the inspector know that Olivia has an identical twin sister?

Is it important to tell the police if you know something about a crime? Why?

How do the police help people in your community?

4
5
Thank you so much, Inspector.
12:10
My pleasure, Miss Jones. And here's your earring.
POLICE DUBLIN STATION
That isn't my earring. I never wear them.
6
Officer, arrest this woman!
What? You can't arrest me. I'm innocent. I've got an alibi.
7
Please explain, Inspector.
12:20
POLICE DUBLIN STATION
I think this woman **is** the thief. I think she **was** at the museum yesterday. I think the woman at the airport was her identical twin sister.
8
Four hours later ...
You were right, Inspector. This is Olga Jones, the twin sister of Olivia Jones.
16:20
The diamond was in her hotel room.
The sisters planned the robbery together. At the airport, Olga said she was Olivia because they wanted you to give Olivia an alibi.
9
Goodbye.
16:55
visit Dublin ZOO
Goodbye, Inspector. Thank you for your help. Now enjoy your holiday.
How did the Inspector know that Olivia had a twin sister? Do you know the answer?

Do you know...?
Identical twins always have different fingerprints.

10 Ask and say.

TALK ABOUT IT!

1 What type of story is *The alibi*?
2 Do you like the story? Why? / Why not?
3 What's your favourite part of the story?
4 Do you like writing stories?

Everyday phrases: learn and use!

My pleasure.
You were right.
Thank you for your help.
Do you know the answer?

GRAMMAR TRACKS

Lesson 4

11 **Listen and read. Act out the dialogues.**

Policeman: Mr Green, **where were you** at **ten past two** yesterday afternoon?
Mr Green: **I was** in the museum souvenir shop.
Policeman: Did you see Olivia Jones?
Mr Green: Yes, I did. She **was** in the shop, talking on her mobile phone. She said, "I've got the diamond. Meet me at the Dragon Hotel in half an hour."

Policewoman: Mrs Brown, **where were you** yesterday afternoon?
Mrs Brown: I **was** in the Dragon Hotel.
Policewoman: Was Olivia Jones in the hotel?
Mrs Brown: Yes, she was. She **was** in the hotel reception at **ten to three**. She **was** with her sister.

12 **Play *Guess the time.***

13  **Listen, repeat and learn.** 

was **and** ***were*** **+** ***at*** **(place) +** ***at*** **(time)**

Where	was he / she	at	10:00	yesterday?
	were you / they		14:00	
			17.45	

I / He / She / It	was	at	the park	at	10:00.
You / We / They	were		school		14:00.
			home		17.45.

I / He / She / It	wasn't	at	the park	at	10:00.
You / We / They	weren't		school		14:00.
			home		17.45.

Was he / she	at home?	Yes,	he / she was.	No,	he / she wasn't.
Were we / they	at the park?		we / they were.		we / they weren't.

14 **Be a grammar detective! Look at page 37 in the AB.**

Do we use *was* and *were* to talk about the past or the future?

Is *five to three* before or after three o'clock?

Is *five past three* before or after three o'clock?

Can you find two examples of the time in the dialogue of the story?

What time is it in each picture of the story? Find the clocks.

FAST TRACK GRAMMAR *Write five sentences about where you were yesterday.*

Lesson 5

15 Listen and identify. Listen and repeat. Point and say.

Sound track /ə/

It's half **past** three.
It's twenty-five **to** four.
It's twenty **to** four.
It's quart**er** **to** four.
It's ten **to** four.
It's five **to** four.
It's four **o'clock**.

a 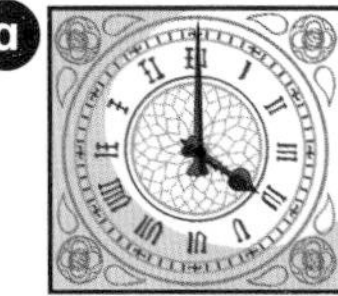
b 
c 
d 
e 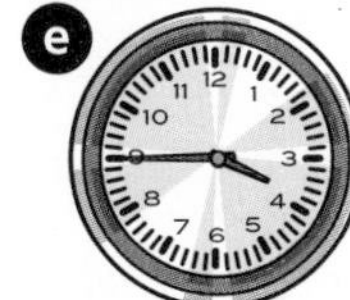
f 
g 

16 Listen and say *True* or *False*. Correct the false sentences.

Clare			Isabel	
Ben				
Sam		Ben		
Isabel	Sam			Clare

17 Play *Where were you?*

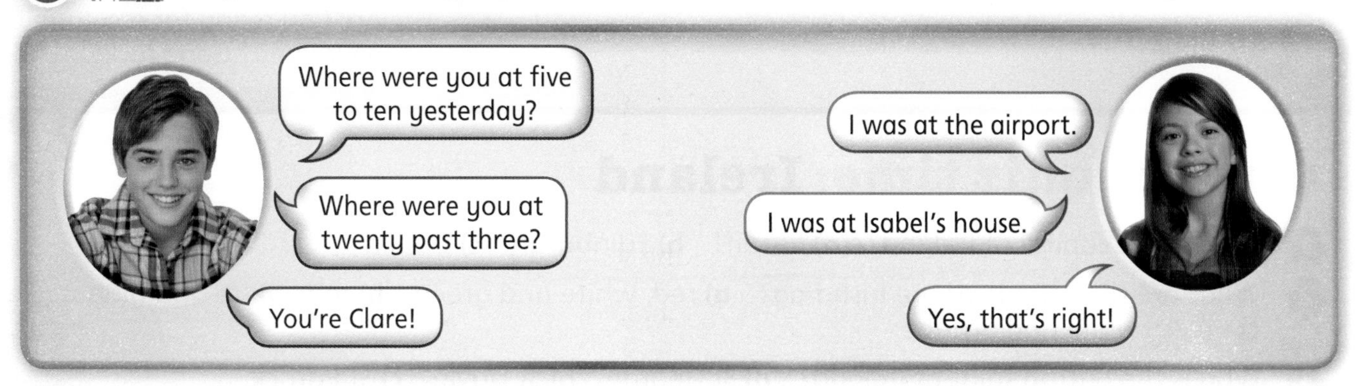

Where were you at five to ten yesterday?
I was at the airport.
Where were you at twenty past three?
I was at Isabel's house.
You're Clare!
Yes, that's right!

18 Talk about where you were yesterday or last Saturday.

Where were you yesterday at quarter past four?

I don't remember. I think I was at a friend's house.

FAST TRACK GRAMMAR *Write five sentences about where your friends were yesterday.*

POST ✓

In Ireland, there are lots of traditional songs which most people know. This article is about one of our most famous songs.

Lesson 6

Listen and read.

Molly Malone

The statue of Molly Malone in Dublin is famous. But who is Molly Malone?

Molly Malone is a character from a traditional song. Almost everyone in Ireland knows the song. Almost everyone in Ireland can sing it. And there are many professional recordings of the song. It is possibly one of the most famous and popular songs in the country.

The song tells Molly's story. She is a beautiful girl who sells fresh seafood in Dublin. She doesn't work in a shop. She sells the seafood from a wheelbarrow.

In Dublin's fair city,
Where the girls are so pretty,
I first set my eyes on sweet Molly Malone,
As she wheeled her wheelbarrow,
Through streets broad and narrow,
Crying "Cockles and mussels, alive, alive, oh!"
"Alive, alive, oh,
Alive, alive, oh",
Crying "Cockles and mussels, alive, alive, oh".

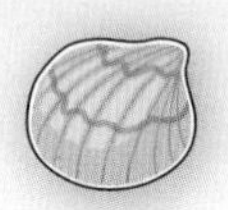

A cockle

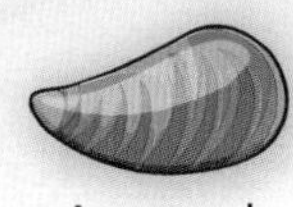

A mussel

Later in the song, Molly dies of a fever. People miss her, but they believe that her ghost continues to walk in the streets of Dublin, crying *Cockles and mussels, alive, alive, oh!*

Who are the most famous characters from books or songs in your country?

Are there any traditional songs in your country which everyone knows?

20 Read and guess. CD2 41 **Listen and say the answers.**

POST ✓

Are you ready for a culture quiz on Ireland? Good luck!

Culture quiz time: Ireland

1. What's the capital of Ireland? **a)** Cardiff **b)** Edinburgh **c)** Dublin
2. What are the colours of the Irish flag? **a)** red, white and green **b)** red, white and blue **c)** green, white and orange
3. Who is the patron saint of Ireland? **a)** St George **b)** St David **c)** St Patrick
4. Which musical instrument is a symbol of Ireland? **a)** a guitar **b)** a harp **c)** a drum
5. What's the most common surname in Ireland? **a)** Murphy **b)** Smith **c)** Jones
6. What type of animal doesn't live in Ireland? **a)** snakes **b)** mosquitoes **c)** pigeons

In the UK, most statues are of real people from history. But some statues are of very famous characters from literature, like Sherlock Holmes.

POST ✓

Lesson 7

21 CD2 43 **Listen and read. Say *True* or *False*.**

1. Sherlock Holmes is a detective from English literature.
2. Sherlock Holmes lives at 212A Baker Street.
3. In his free time, Sherlock plays the drums.
4. 221B Baker Street is now the address of the Sherlock Holmes Museum.
5. There is a souvenir shop at the museum.
6. There is a statue of Sherlock Holmes outside Baker Street underground station.

Everyday chit-chat

! How to find out about opening and closing times

22 CD3 1 **Listen and repeat.**

1 information

2 wheelchair access

3 lift

4 restaurant

23 CD3 2 **Listen and read. Repeat.** 

Woman: Good morning. This is the Tourist Information Office. How can I help you?
Ed: Hello. Can you tell me what time the Science Museum opens on Saturdays, please?
Woman: It opens at 10 o'clock in the morning. It closes at 6 o'clock in the evening.
Ed: Does it close for lunch?
Woman: No, it's open all day. And there are cafés and restaurants in the museum.
Ed: Are there any special exhibitions on this month?
Woman: Yes. There's an exhibition about robots. You can find information about it on the museum website.
Ed: One last question. Is there wheelchair access?
Woman: Yes, there is. The wheelchair access is very good and there are lifts to every floor.
Ed: Thank you very much.
Woman: You're welcome.

24 **Do a role play.**

ICT

Lesson 8

Listen and read.

I'm not very techy but I use a computer program to create my comic strips. This article is about how other people from Dublin use technology. POST ✓

TECHNOLOGY in the city

Technology plays an important part in our lives today. Five people from Dublin tell us how they use technology in the city.

1. SATNAV

I'm a taxi driver in Dublin. I've got satnav in the taxi. I use it to find addresses in the city. It also tells me if there are any traffic problems. Satnav technology makes my job a lot easier.

2. TABLETS

We use a tablet to go online. We look up the opening times of shops and museums. We also find out what's on at the cinema and what time the films start. It's easier, cheaper and quicker than a phone call.

3. WIFI ZONES & LAPTOPS

I'm lucky. I've got a small laptop. I use it to send emails and to chat to my friends. I can now do those things in the city centre because there are lots of places with free wifi zones: cafés, the library, parks, etc. I like using my laptop in the park. I can do my homework and get fresh air at the same time!

4. APPS & SMARTPHONES

I'm learning French. I haven't got much time to practise. But now I'm learning words and expressions with an app on my smartphone. It's great because I can use it anywhere in the city.

5. ONLINE SHOPPING

I love online shopping. I send my shopping list to the supermarket and they deliver everything to my house. It's so easy and it saves me lots of time.

CAN YOU IMAGINE YOUR LIFE WITHOUT TECHNOLOGY?

26 Read and complete the sentences.

1. He likes using satnav because it…
2. They use a tablet to…
3. He uses wifi zones and his laptop to…
4. She uses an app on her smartphone to…
5. She does online shopping because it…

27 Play *Five reasons why.*

Smartphone.
A smartphone is useful because you can take photos.

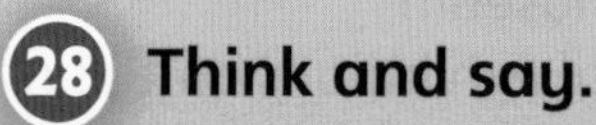

A smartphone is useful because you can take photos and send text messages.

28 Think and say.

How does technology affect your life?
Which electronic gadgets do you use at home and at school?

My words to remember
wifi zone online shopping app go online chat smartphone

These words are abbreviations: *www, satnav, app.* Find out what they stand for.

Project: A guide for tourists

29 Listen and read.

Read my project about Liverpool. What can you see from the top of the Echo Wheel? What time does Sefton Park close?

POST ✓

Places to visit in Liverpool

Liverpool is a city in the north west of England. I was there last August. Here are two places I can recommend.

The Echo Wheel is a very popular tourist attraction in Liverpool. It's 60 metres tall. I recommend the wheel because you can see incredible views of the city. From the top of the wheel you can see parks, museums and galleries. You can see the river Mersey. On a clear day, you can see the mountains in Wales. The wheel turns 360° and the ride lasts about 15 minutes. Check online for ticket prices and opening times. The wheel has got wheelchair access.

Sefton Park is one of Liverpool's largest green areas. I recommend the park because it's the perfect place for a quiet walk or a bike ride. There are statues and fountains in the park. There's a lake where you can rent a boat. For sporty people, there are areas where you can play tennis, football and other sports. If you want to take your laptop, there are cafés with wifi zones. The park is open 24 hours a day and it's free to go in.

By Becky

30 Plan your project.

THINKING SKILLS
Explaining

1. Choose a village, town or city you know.
2. Find out about places to visit.
3. Find out about the opening times.
4. Write and present your recommendations.

You can also present your project in this way.

This is a photo of Sefton Park. It is one of the biggest parks in Liverpool.

➔ AB page 42

Do the Unit 4 Review and Self-assessment (Activity Book page 42). Complete your *Progress Journal* for Unit 4.

Ingenious inventions

In this unit:

- I **name** and **talk about** inventions.
- I **listen to** and **read** a true story *The discovery of vaccination.*
- I **ask** and **answer** questions about people's lives in the past.
- I **find out about** English and UK culture.
- I **act out** talking about what I did at school in a role play.
- I **read about** the history of an invention, and **write** and **present** a project.

Lesson 1

1 Listen and say. 

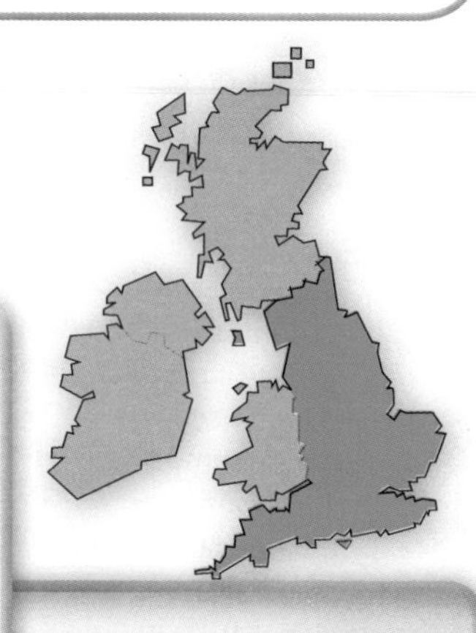

Tiger Tracks SLN POST

Hi. I'm Becky. I live in Manchester, in England. My favourite subjects at school are history and science. I'm especially interested in the history of things we use every day. One of these inventions is from England. Do you know which one? Do you know how old these inventions are?

1 light bulb

2 stamps

3 umbrella

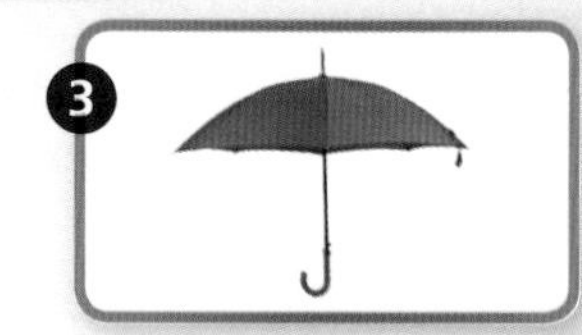

4 dishwasher

5 plasters

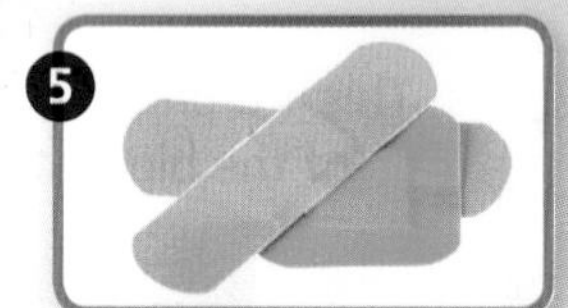

6 paper clip

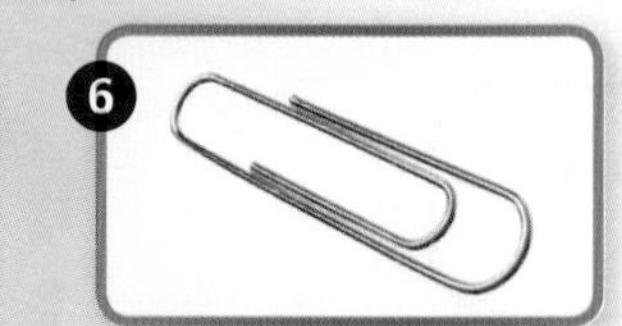

7 microwave

8 microscope

9 bilingual dictionary

10 digital thermometer

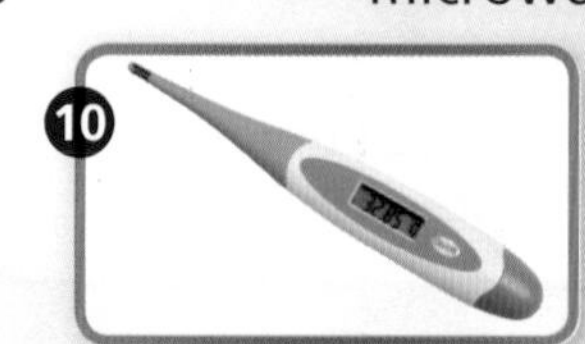

2 Discuss with a partner. Write your ideas. Now listen and find out.

How old is the light bulb?

It's more than 200 years old.

It's between 100 and 200 years old.

It's less than 100 years old.

3 Listen and do the vocabulary quiz.

You use this when you learn a foreign language.

INTERNET TRACKS Find out the name of the first stamp in the world.

Lesson 2

4 **Listen and read.**

POST ✓

I love finding out about great scientists and inventors from history. Here are four mini-biographies about four of my favourite inventors. Which do you think is the most interesting?

READING TIP: Use the pictures to help you understand the text.

Four Inventors

Leonardo da Vinci (1452 – 1519)

Leonardo da Vinci painted the Mona Lisa, which is perhaps the most famous painting in the world. But Leonardo was also a scientist and an inventor. He invented some musical instruments and a type of clock. He also designed this flying machine.

Josephine Cochrane (1839 – 1913)

In about 1880, Josephine Cochrane had an idea. She wanted to design a machine to wash dishes. So she studied science and mechanics. She learned how to draw. She worked on her design for six years. Finally, in 1886, her dishwashing machine was complete.

Thomas Edison (1847 – 1931)

Thomas Edison invented many things. He invented the phonograph (a machine for recording sound), a type of battery and a type of car. But his most famous invention was a type of light bulb. He was not the first person to invent a light bulb, but his design was the most efficient. Nowadays, there are light bulbs for bicycles, mobile phones, fridges and microscopes. Can you imagine life without light bulbs?

George Lerner (1922 – 1995)

In 1949, George Lerner invented a plastic toy called Mr Potato Head. At first, the toy was not a success. But in 1952, Mr Potato Head appeared in a television commercial. Then every child wanted the toy. Today, Mr Potato Head is one of the most popular toys in the world. He is also a character in the *Toy Story* films.

THINKING SKILLS
Sequencing

5 **Put these events in chronological order.**

- Leonardo da Vinci painted the Mona Lisa.
- Mr Potato Head appeared on television.
- Thomas Edison died.
- Josephine Cochrane invented the first dishwasher.

6 **Play a memory game.**

Who invented a type of clock?

Leonardo da Vinci.

Yes, that's right!

7 **Think and say.**

I think two of the greatest inventions are the mobile phone and the car.

INTERNET TRACKS Think of an object you use every day. Try to find out who invented it.

Lesson 3

8 CD3 13 **Listen to and read the story.**

POST ✓

This is a true story about one of my favourite scientists. It's the story of one of the most important discoveries in history. I hope you like it.

The discovery of vaccination

- **What was smallpox?**
- **What did Edward Jenner discover?**

In the 18th century, a terrible disease called smallpox killed 10% of the population every year. It killed men, women and children. It killed rich people and poor people. It killed kings and queens.

1

In 1796, Edward Jenner was a doctor. He worked in a small village in England.

I've got a headache and lots of spots. I think I've got smallpox.

2

Where do you work?

I work on a farm. I milk the cows.

Have the cows got spots?

Yes, they have.

3

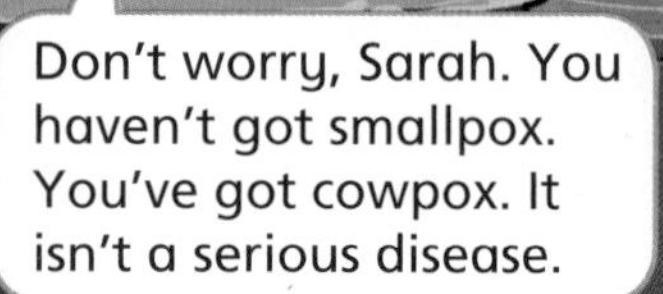

Don't worry, Sarah. You haven't got smallpox. You've got cowpox. It isn't a serious disease.

4

Jenner noticed that people who got cowpox didn't get smallpox.

5

Jenner asked a boy from the village to do an experiment with him. He rubbed pus from one of Sarah's spots into a scratch on the boy's arm.

9 **Read and say *True* or *False*. Correct the false sentences.**

1. Edward Jenner was a doctor in a large city.
2. Sarah worked on a farm with horses.
3. Cowpox can't kill you.
4. The boy didn't get cowpox.
5. The Latin word for cow is vaccination.
6. Cowpox is more serious than smallpox.

Is it important to prevent illness and disease? Why?

What do you do to prevent illness?

5

6
Four days later ...
I've got a headache, doctor. I've got a fever and lots of spots.
When did it start?
Yesterday.
Don't worry. You've got cowpox. It isn't serious.
Ten days later ...
I'm feeling better.

7
In the second part of the experiment, Jenner rubbed pus from a smallpox patient into a scratch on the boy's arm.
I don't want to get smallpox.
Don't worry.

8

One week later ...

I haven't got spots or any symptoms of smallpox.

This proves that cowpox protects people from smallpox.

9

Jenner repeated the experiment with many people. He always got the same result.

The word for cow in Latin is vacca...
vacca
vaccination
...so I call this treatment vaccination.

Do you know...?
The last case of smallpox was in 1977.

Doctors continued to use and develop Jenner's vaccination theories. Today there aren't any cases of smallpox in the world, and vaccination is used against many other diseases.

10

10 Ask and say.

TALK ABOUT IT!

1 Do you like the story? Why? / Why not?
2 What's your favourite part of the story?
3 Do you think Jenner was a good doctor?
4 Do you think Sarah and the boy were brave?

Everyday phrases: learn and use!

What's the matter?
Don't worry.
It isn't serious.
I'm feeling better.

Lesson 4

Listen and read.

What do we know about Edward Jenner?

We know that Edward Jenner was a brilliant doctor and scientist. He developed a treatment to protect patients from smallpox. He saved the lives of many people. But **where did he live? What did he do** in his free time? **Did he have** a family? **When did he die?**

Edward Jenner lived from 1749 to 1823. He lived with his wife and three children in a small village in England called Berkeley. He often treated people at his home, but he didn't take any money from poor people.

Jenner had many hobbies. He was very interested in wildlife. In his free time, he liked watching birds and hedgehogs.

Jenner was also interested in hot air balloons, because they were a very new invention. In 1784, more than 100 years before the invention of the plane, Jenner travelled nearly 40 kilometres in a balloon.

Today, Edward Jenner's home is a museum about his life and his interests.

  **Play *Read and change.***

Edward Jenner was a brilliant farmer.

Stop. It doesn't say farmer. It says doctor.

 **Listen, repeat and learn.** 

***Wh-* questions in the past**

Did	you / he / they	live in England? discover vaccination? have a family?	Yes,	you / he / they did.	No,	you / he / they didn't.

Where What When	did	you / he / they	live? do? die?

14 Be a grammar detective! Look at page 47 in the AB.

What are the short answers to questions beginning with *Did you…?*

How many *Wh-* question words do you know?

Can you find an example of a *Wh-* question in the past in the story?

FAST TRACK GRAMMAR *Write five* Wh- *questions about a famous inventor.*

Lesson 5

Sound track

15 Listen and identify the differences. Listen and repeat.

I live at home.
I work at school.
I play at the weekend.
I want to travel round the world.
I invent machines.

I lived at home.
I worked at school.
I played at the weekend.
I wanted to travel round the world.
I invented machines.

16 Listen and answer the questions.

Earle Dickson
1892 – 1961

Place: USA
Profession: inventor
Invention: plasters

Marie Curie
1876 – 1934

Place: France
Profession: scientist
Discovery: an element called radium

Walter Frederick Morrison
1920 – 2010

Place: USA
Profession: inventor
Invention: the Frisbee

17 Do three role plays.

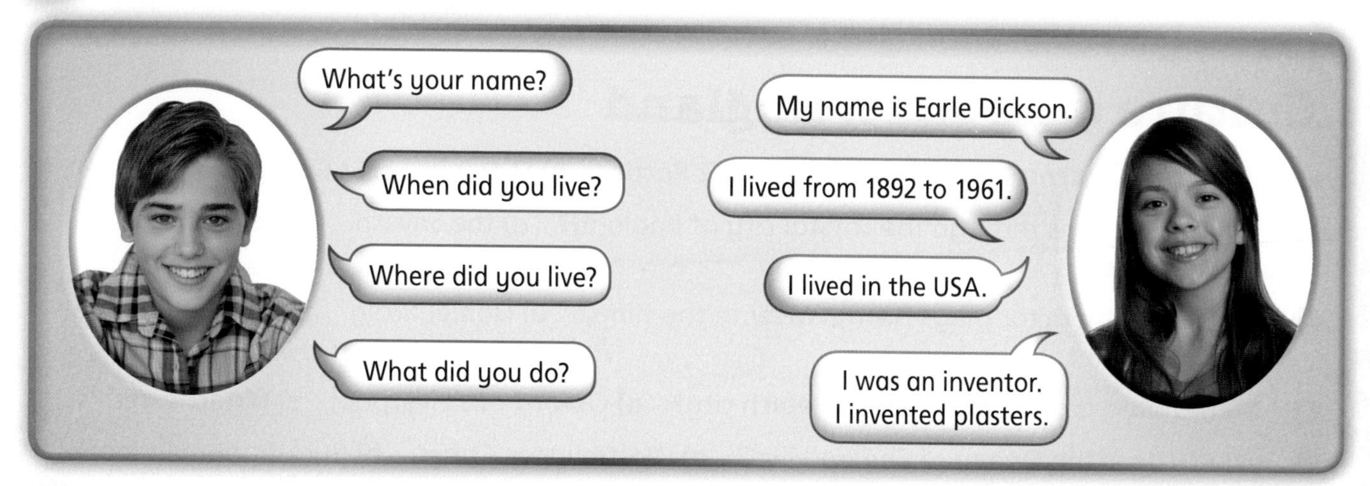

What's your name?
My name is Earle Dickson.
When did you live?
I lived from 1892 to 1961.
Where did you live?
I lived in the USA.
What did you do?
I was an inventor. I invented plasters.

18 Act out one of the role plays for your friends.

FAST TRACK GRAMMAR *Write a dialogue about Marie Curie. Use* What, When *and* Where.

One of my favourite places to visit is in Cornwall, in the south west of England. It's called the Eden Project. It's a great place to learn about natural science.

POST ✓

Lesson 6

19 CD3 20 **Listen and read.**

The Eden Project

An amazing place to visit

These buildings are called biomes. Inside, you can see trees and plants that normally grow in other countries. In the Mediterranean biome you can see lemon, orange and olive trees. In the Rainforest biome there are waterfalls, and you can see banana, cacao, and chewing gum trees. If you're observant, you can also see tree frogs, butterflies, lizards and birds.

The Eden Project isn't just a garden. It teaches people about plants. There are information sheets that explain why many of the plants are important. The Eden Project gardeners also give lessons on gardening. They can teach you how to grow vegetables at home.

There are many other reasons to go to the Eden Project. There's an ice rink in winter, there's a rock climbing club, and there are beautiful sculptures in the gardens. And if you like adventure sports, you can go on the longest zip wire in England!

For more information on the Eden Project, why don't you visit the Eden Project website?

Is there a place like the Eden Project in your country?
What's your favourite place to visit?

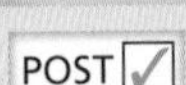

20 **Read and guess.** CD3 21 **Listen and say the answers.**

POST ✓

How much do you know about England? Are you ready for the culture quiz?

Culture quiz time: England

1. Who is the patron saint of England? a) St Patrick b) St David c) St George
2. Which river runs through the capital city of England? a) the Severn b) the Thames c) the Mersey
3. Which English actor plays Harry Potter in the films? a) Daniel Craig b) Daniel Radcliffe c) Rupert Grint
4. Man United is a football team in which city? a) Oxford b) Liverpool c) Manchester
5. Where does the Queen of England live? a) Westminster Abbey b) Buckingham Palace c) The Tower of London
6. What's the national sport of England? a) cricket b) tennis c) rollerskating

Do you like doing science projects at school? In the UK there is a national competition for the best science project. POST✓

Lesson 7

21 CD3 23 **Listen and read. Say *True* or *False*.**

1 The National Science + Engineering Competition is every year.
2 The competition is for young people between 11 and 21 years old.
3 You can't enter a maths project in the competition.
4 You can enter the competition as a team or as an individual.
5 The competition takes place all over the UK, and the final is in London.
6 The winning projects receive a prize.

Everyday chit-chat

! How to talk about what you did at school

22 CD3 24 **Listen and repeat.**

the 19th century

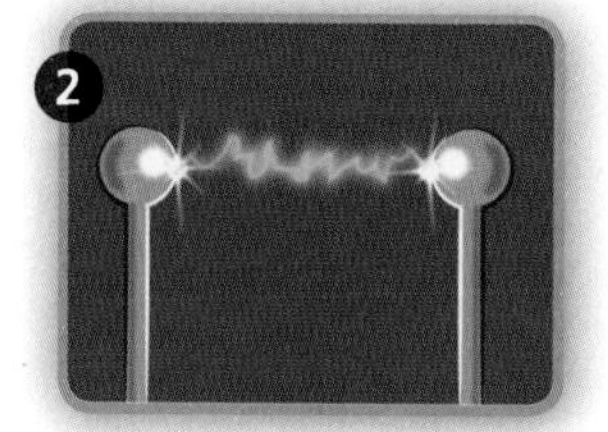

electricity

batteries

an idea

23 CD3 25 **Listen and read. Repeat.** video

Dad: What did you do at school today?
Ed: Lots of things. Art, maths, science and Spanish. And we started a history project.
Dad: A project! What's it about?
Ed: It's about the invention of machines in the 19th century. It's really interesting. I like history.
Dad: What did you learn in science?
Ed: Something about batteries and electricity. I didn't really understand it. It was very complicated.
Dad: Well, why don't we go to the Science Museum at the weekend? The museum always explains things simply.
Ed: That's a great idea. Can I ask a friend to come with us?
Dad: Of course.

24 **Do a role play.**

History

Lesson 8

POST

Hi there! I think television is an amazing invention. This timeline shows the development of television in the UK.

25 Listen and read.

The history of television in the UK

At the beginning of the 20th century television didn't exist. In the evenings, people talked and played games. They looked at books. Some people played musical instruments. After 1920, some people listened to the radio. Life was very different.

In the 1930s, there were two hours of television programmes every day in the UK. But most people didn't have a television at home. Television wasn't popular. People preferred the radio.

In 1953, lots of people wanted to buy a television because they wanted to watch the coronation of Queen Elizabeth II. Suddenly, television was popular.

In 1967, for the first time, some television programmes were in colour.

In 2000, 96% of homes in the UK had at least one television.

1900 — 2000

In 1926, a Scottish engineer called John Logie Baird demonstrated the first working television in the UK. The images on the screen were in black and white, and they weren't very clear, but it was an important moment in the development of television technology.

Today, in the 21st century, televisions are bigger and better than in the past. They've got flat screens and the image is very clear. There are many different channels and many different types of programme to watch. We can also watch television programmes on our computers, tablets and smartphones. Some people think we now watch too much television. What do you think?

26 Put the events in chronological order.

- Some progammes were in colour for the first time.
- People watched the coronation of Queen Elizabeth II.
- 96% of houses had a television.
- Televisions didn't exist.
- There were two hours of programmes every day.
- A Scottish engineer demonstrated a type of television.

27 Play *True or False?*

John Logie Baird was English.

False. He was Scottish.

28 Think and say.

Is television important to you? Why? How much time do you spend watching television?

My words to remember

image flat screen clear
television programmes channels
at the beginning of the 20th century

Find out about John Logie Baird. When and where did he live?

Project: Inventions

29 Listen and read.

Last week at school, we did a project about inventions. I wrote this timeline about the invention of the train. How old is the train? POST ✓

Trains

At the beginning of the 19th century, trains didn't exist. People travelled by horse and cart. They needed more than a day to travel 150 kilometres.

In 1814, an English engineer called George Stephenson invented a locomotive. It pulled 30 tons of coal up a hill. It travelled at six kilometres an hour. It was the best locomotive of the time.

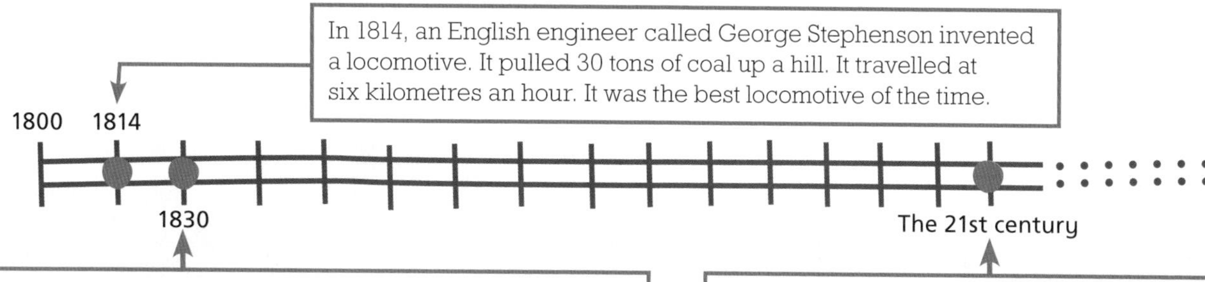

George Stephenson also designed the first train line for passengers. The line opened in September 1830. It transported people from Manchester to Liverpool. George and his son, Robert Stephenson, designed a famous locomotive for the line. It was called Stephenson's Rocket. You can see it in the Science Museum in London.

Stephenson's Rocket

Today, in the 21st century, trains are longer, faster and more comfortable than in the past. There are high-speed trains that travel at more than 400 kilometres an hour. 400 kilometres an hour! That's very fast!

A high-speed train

I think the train is a great invention. Trains save us lots of time. We can travel to other cities and countries by train. And trains are more ecological than cars. Can you imagine life without trains?

by Ed

30 Plan your project.

THINKING SKILLS
Contrasting

1. Think of an invention. Find out who invented it and when.
2. Think about life before and after the invention. What did people do before the invention? Do people use the invention today? How?
3. Do you think it is a great invention? Why? Why not?
4. Write and present your project.

You can also present your project in this way.

Today, modern trains are very fast and comfortable.

→ AB page 52

Do the Unit 5 Review and Self-assessment (Activity Book page 52). Complete your *Progress Journal* for Unit 5.

6 Helping people

AIMS

In this unit:

- I **name** and **talk about** chores.
- I **listen to** and **read** a modern fairy tale *The red running shoes.*
- I **ask** and **answer** questions about what I did and didn't do in the past.
- I **find out about** Canadian and UK culture.
- I **act out** asking for and giving directions in a role play.
- I **read about** children who help other people, and **write** and **present** a project.

Lesson 1

1 CD3 30 **Listen and say.** 

Tiger Tracks SLN

POST

Hi. My name's Zoe. I live in Toronto, in Canada. At home, everyone in my family helps to do the housework. Which of these chores do you think I do? Who does these chores in your home?

1 do the washing up

2 put your clothes away

3 make your bed

4 tidy up

5 clean the windows

6 take out the rubbish

7 feed the pets

8 water the plants

9 sweep the floor

10 wash the car

2 CD3 31 **Listen and find out. Which chores does Zoe do? Now ask and talk about you.**

Who makes your bed?

I usually do.

My mother / father / brother / sister does.

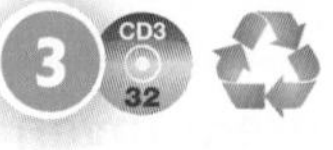

3 CD3 32 **Listen and do the vocabulary quiz. Say the missing words**

Everyone helps to ___ up in my house. We do it together.

INTERNET TRACKS Find a map of Canada. Is it bigger or smaller than the USA?

Lesson 2

 **Listen and read.**

My mother is an ice hockey champion. She needs to train and practise for many hours every day. My dad, my brother and I help do the chores. This is a typical day for my family. Is it similar in your family? POST ✓

Life in my family

From Monday to Friday, my mother gets up at quarter to six in the morning. She has a banana and some fruit juice and then she runs 10 kilometres. I get up at quarter past seven with my dad and my little brother. I have a shower and get dressed. And then the whole family has breakfast together at half past seven.

When my brother and I go to school, my mother goes to work. She has a part-time job in a laboratory. In the afternoon, she goes to a sports centre with an ice rink. At the sports centre she meets the other members of the ice hockey team. Sometimes they work with a professional trainer in the gym, and sometimes they work with their coach on the ice.

After school, my brother and I usually do some chores. We tidy up. I take out the rubbish. My brother feeds the cat and waters the plants. Our dad does the cooking. He likes cooking. He always prepares tasty food that is good for us. When my mum comes home at six o'clock, the house is tidy and dinner is ready. We always have dinner together, and we talk about what we did at school.

Last weekend, my mother played an important match. Her team didn't win, but she scored lots of goals. I took this photo! My brother and I are very proud of our mother.

You don't need to read every word to find the information you want.

5 Answer the questions.

1. Who waters the plants?
2. Who takes out the rubbish?
3. Who prepares the food?
4. Who works in a laboratory?
5. Who comes home at six o'clock?

 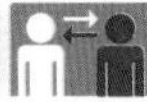 **Play a memory game.**

THINKING SKILLS
Remembering

Who feeds the cat?

Zoe's brother does.

TALK ABOUT IT!

7 Think and say.

At home, I do the washing up and I sweep the floor. I don't really like doing chores, but I think it's important to help.

 **INTERNET TRACKS** Find out how many people are in an ice hockey team.

Lesson 3

Listen to and read the story.

When I was younger, I liked traditional fairy tales. Now I'm older, I prefer modern fairy tales. This one is set in Canada. Enjoy! ☺

The red running shoes

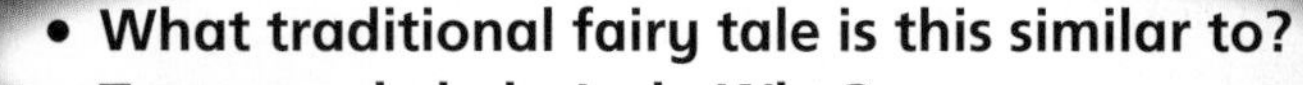

- **What traditional fairy tale is this similar to?**
- **Two people help Josh. Who?**

1 **Once upon a time, there was a boy called Josh. He lived in Canada with his stepfather and his two stepsisters.**

2 **Josh dreamed of winning marathons. But on the day of the marathon in his town, his stepsisters took his running shoes.**

3 **Josh was very unhappy.**

Don't forget to do the washing up.

And remember to clean the windows.

4 **Then suddenly there was a flash!**

Don't be sad, Josh. I am your fairy godfather. I am here to help you.

5 **The fairy godfather waved his magic wand, and suddenly Josh was in different clothes.**

9 **Read and answer the questions.**

1. Where did Josh live?
2. Were his stepsisters kind to Josh?
3. What did the fairy godfather give Josh?
4. Who did the washing up on the day of the marathon?
5. Was Josh the fastest runner in the marathon?
6. What is Josh doing now?

Is it important to share housework? Why?

Do you and your family share the chores?

6 Josh joined the other runners on the starting line.

And the fairy godfather did the washing up, made the beds and took out the rubbish.

7 Josh was the first runner to finish the marathon.

The boy in red is the winner!
Who is he?
I don't know.

8 Josh didn't want his stepsisters and the photographers to see him. He ran home.

9 One week later, an athletics coach visited Josh's house. He put the running shoe on Josh's foot.

The shoe fits! You are the winner of the marathon!

10 Now, Josh is training for the next Olympics. And his stepsisters do their own cleaning.

Do you know...?
A marathon is 42.195 kilometres long. The fastest marathon runners can complete the race in less than two and a half hours!

10 Ask and say.

1 Do you like the story? Why? / Why not?
2 What's your favourite part of the story?
3 Has the story got a happy ending?
4 Do you know any other modern fairy stories?

Everyday phrases: learn and use!

Don't be sad.
I am here to help you.
Don't forget to do the washing up.
Be home before 12 o'clock.

GRAMMAR TRACKS

Lesson 4

Listen to and read the poem.

She isn't at home.
Take me back to the palace, please.

A visit from the Queen

Yesterday morning I **did** some chores.
I **made** the beds and I **swept** the floors.
I wanted the house to be very clean
For a visit from Her Majesty the Queen.

I **took** out the rubbish in the afternoon.
I **put** things away and I tidied my room.
I wanted the house to be very clean
For a visit from Her Majesty the Queen.

But when the Queen arrived for tea,
At exactly quarter past three,
I didn't hear her knock at the door.
You see, I **was** exhausted from too many chores.
I **was** asleep in my rocking chair
And Her Majesty the Queen **thought** I wasn't there.

12 **Work in groups. Play *Team reading race*.**

Yesterday morning I did some chores.

I made the beds and I swept the floors.

Listen, repeat and learn. 

Irregular verbs in the past

Every day

I / You / We / They	take out the rubbish. feed the dog.
He / She	does the washing up.

I / You / We / They	don't	take out the rubbish. feed the dog.
He / She	doesn't	do the washing up.

Yesterday

I / You / We / They	took out the rubbish. fed the dog.
He / She	did the washing up.

I / You / We / They	didn't	take out the rubbish. feed the dog.
He / She	didn't	do the washing up.

Did	you / he / they	feed the dog? sweep the floor?	Yes,	I / you / he / they did.	No,	I / you / he / they didn't.

14 **Be a grammar detective! Look at page 57 in the AB.**

Can you remember how to form a **regular** verb in the past?

Is there a rule to help you form **irregular** verbs in the past?

How many regular and irregular verbs can you find in the story?

FAST TRACK GRAMMAR *Start an irregular verb list in your notebook.*

Lesson 5

Sound track

15 CD3 39 **Guess the end of the sentences. Listen and check. Listen and repeat.**

She didn't clean the windows, …	I didn't finish my geography test, …	She didn't win, …

… but she scored a goal.	… but she swept the floors.	… but I got a good mark.

16 CD3 40 **Listen and say *True* or *False*. Correct the false sentences.**

Ruth	✓	✗	✗	✓	✗	✓
Daniel	✗	✓	✓	✗	✓	✗
Emma	✓	✓	✗	✗	✓	✗
Duncan	✗	✗	✓	✓	✗	✓

17 **Play *Who am I?***

Did you take out the rubbish yesterday?
Yes, I did. And I made my bed.
Did you do the washing up?
No, I didn't. But I fed the dog.
You're Emma!
Yes, that's right!

18 **Ask and say what you did yesterday.**

Did you do any chores yesterday?

Yes, I did. I put my clothes away.

FAST TRACK GRAMMAR *Write five sentences about what you did and didn't do yesterday.*

Sport is an important part of Canadian culture. Winter sports are especially popular. And almost everyone in Canada loves watching the Winter Olympics. POST ✓

Lesson 6

19 CD3 42 **Listen and read.**

Canada at the Winter Olympics

The Winter Olympics take place once every four years. Sports at the Winter Olympics include skiing, skating, ice hockey and snowboarding. These are sports that need ice and snow.

Canadians are passionate about ice hockey. It's their national winter sport. Skiing and skating are also very popular in Canada. So Canadians are always very interested in the Winter Olympics. The country usually does very well.

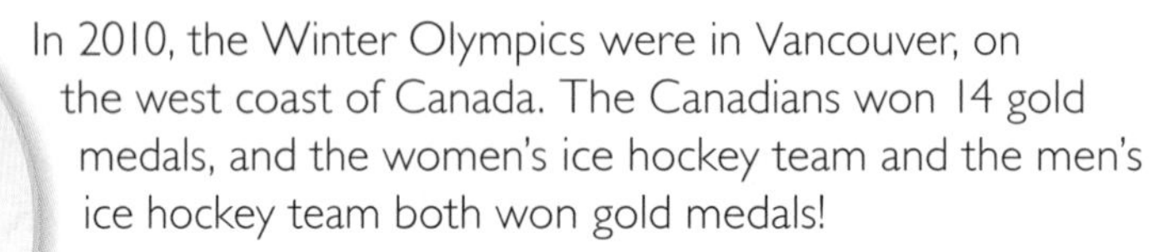

In 2010, the Winter Olympics were in Vancouver, on the west coast of Canada. The Canadians won 14 gold medals, and the women's ice hockey team and the men's ice hockey team both won gold medals!

Tessa Virtue and Scott Moir were the ice dance Champions at the 2010 Winter Olympics. They were the youngest people to win an Olympic gold medal in the history of their sport!

Are there any famous sportsmen and women in your country? What sports are popular in your country?

20 **Read and guess.** CD3 43 **Listen and say the answers.**

How much do you know about Canada? Are you ready for the culture quiz? POST ✓

Culture quiz time: Canada

1. What's the capital of Canada? a) Ottawa b) Toronto c) Montreal
2. What's the largest city in Canada? a) Ottawa b) Toronto c) Montreal
3. What can you see on the flag of Canada? a) a red bird b) a red flower c) a red leaf
4. Which language isn't an official language of Canada? a) English b) French c) Spanish
5. Which famous waterfalls are in Canada? a) Victoria Falls b) Niagara Falls c) Angel Falls
6. Canada is the second largest country in the world. How big is it? a) about 13 million km² b) about 10 million km² c) about 6 million km²

The 2012 Summer Olympics were in London. They were incredible. I loved watching all the different sports. POST

Lesson 7

21 Listen and read. Say *True* or *False*.

1 The Olympic Park is in West London.
2 The park includes a stadium and an aquatics centre.
3 Exactly 200 countries participated in the games.
4 More than 10,000 athletes participated in the games.
5 The British team won 75 medals: 29 gold, 17 silver and 19 bronze.
6 The UK post office printed stamps of all the UK Olympic champions.

Everyday chit-chat

How to ask for and give directions

22 Listen and repeat.

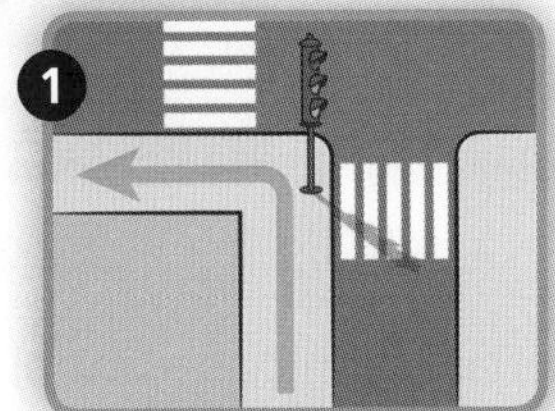

1 turn left at the traffic lights

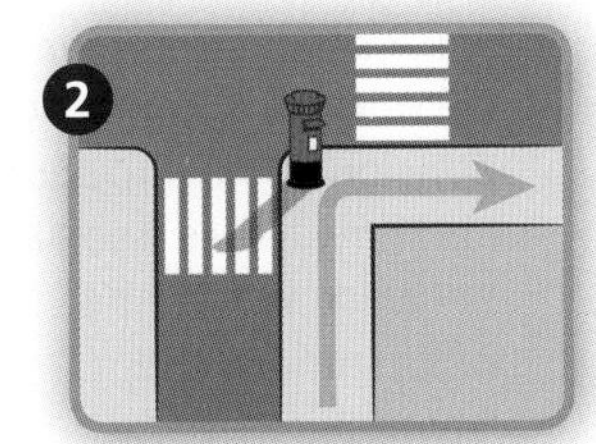

2 turn right at the post box

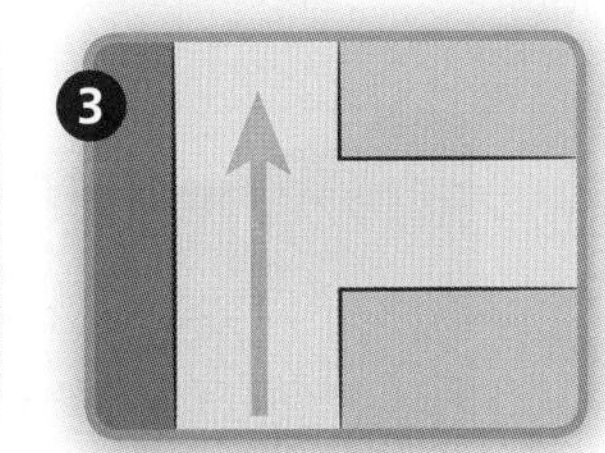

3 go straight on

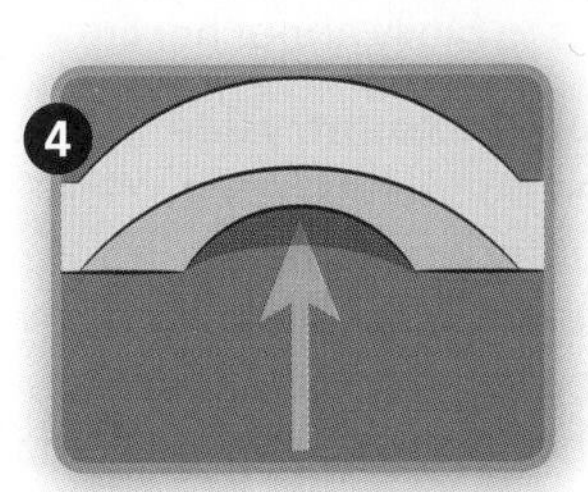

4 go under the bridge

23 Listen and read. Repeat.

Ed: Hello. You look lost. Can I help you?
Woman: Do you know the way to the sports stadium?
Ed: Yes. It's very near here. Go straight on and turn left at the traffic lights.
Woman: Left at the traffic lights.
Ed: Then go straight on and go under the bridge.
Woman: Under the bridge.
Ed: After the bridge, turn right at the post box.
Woman: Right at the post box.
Ed: And then the sports stadium is on your left. OK?
Woman: I'm sorry. I'm French and my English is not very good. Can you repeat it?
Ed: I can show you the way. It isn't far.
Woman: Oh. OK. That's very kind of you. Thank you.
Ed: It's this way.

24 Do a role play.

Lesson 8

25 Listen and read.

I'm very sporty. Every Saturday I work as volunteer at a sports club for young children. I help the adults monitor the children. It's fun. This webpage explains how teenagers around the world help other people. POST

Children and teenagers in action

All around the world, children and teenagers are helping to make their communities better places. They give up their free time to help neighbours and charity organisations. Their actions improve many people's lives.

Help an elderly neighbour
This is Gemma. She lives with her family in Michigan in the USA. Their neighbour, Molly, is 86 years old. Gemma visits Molly every day and offers help. She sweeps her garden path and waters her plants. And she talks to Molly about her life at school.

Clean up the countryside
Nick and his friends help to clean up the countryside in the UK. They meet at the weekend once a month. They go to rivers, beaches, parks and forests to pick up all the litter they can find. Sometimes they have competitions to see who can find the most litter.

Walk dogs
Leroy and his younger sister are volunteer dog walkers. Every weekend they go to a charity for abandoned dogs in Dublin. They take the dogs for walks in the park or in the countryside. They also help to train the dogs.

Visit a retirement home
Lisa's favourite subject is ICT. She's good with computers. So, once a week she visits a retirement home in Wellington. She teaches the pensioners how to send emails and how to use a social network. With Lisa's help, some of the pensioners are writing blogs.

Can you do more to help people in your community?

THINKING SKILLS
Analysing

26 **Read, think and answer.**

What is a good way to help people in your community...
...if you're very techy?
...if you like walking?
...if you like the countryside?
...if you like chatting to people?
...if you like animals?

27 **Play *Question challenge*.**

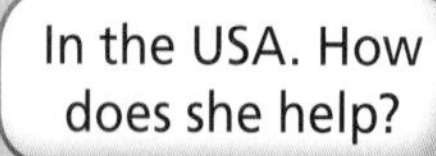

Where does Gemma live?

In the USA. How does she help?

She visits an elderly neighbour called Molly. How often does she visit Molly?

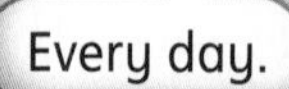

Every day.

28 **Think and say.**

Do you help people in your community?
Can you think of new ways to help people in your community?

My words to remember

retirement home, charity, pick up litter, elderly neighbour, walk the dog, pensioner

INTERNET TRACKS Find out the full names of these charities: RSPCA, RSPB and NSPCC. What do they do?

Project: How we can help

29 Listen and read.

This is a project we did at school. Do you like my ideas for helping? POST ✓

How I help people at home

I live with my mother and father, my little brother and our dog, Buster. At home I often help my parents do the chores. I always make my bed and put my things away. I sometimes take out the rubbish. I feed and walk our dog. I never do the washing up because we've got a dishwasher. But I take the dishes out of the dishwasher and my mother puts them away.

How I helped people last week

Last week, I helped my grandmother to use the computer. And I helped my mother to carry bags of shopping from the supermarket. At school, I tidied the bookshelves in our English classroom, and I picked up litter from the playground.

My ideas for helping people in our community

IDEA 1

We all have toys that we don't want. I think we can put all our unwanted toys in boxes and give them to a children's hospital.

FOR THE CHILDREN'S HOSPITAL

IDEA 2

We all have books we don't need any more. We can organise a book sale at school. We can give the money we raise to charity.

GIVE A COIN TAKE A BOOK ALL MONEY FOR CHARITY
50
£1

by Becky

30 Plan your project.

THINKING SKILLS
Analysing

1. How do you help at home?
2. How did you help people last week?
3. How can your class help the community?
4. Write and present your project.

You can also present your project in this way.

Last week, I helped my grandmother to use the computer.

➔ AB page 62

Do the Unit 6 Review and Self-assessment (Activity Book page 62). Complete your *Progress Journal* for Unit 6.

7 A camping trip

In this unit:

- I **name** and **describe** camping equipment.
- I **listen to** and **read** a photo story *The tiger thieves.*
- I **talk about** plans in the future.
- I **find out about** places to visit in Yorkshire.
- I **talk about** going to secondary school in a role play.
- I **read about** dramatic weather, and **write** and **present** a project.

Lesson 1

1 CD4 5 **Listen and say.** 

Tiger Tracks SLN POST

Hi, everyone – Ed here. I'm going to go camping in Yorkshire, in the north of England, with Scott, Florence, Finn, Becky and Zoe. Which of these things do you think I need to take? Can you think of anything else I need?

1 
waterproof jacket

2 
blanket

3 sleeping bag

4 
tent

5 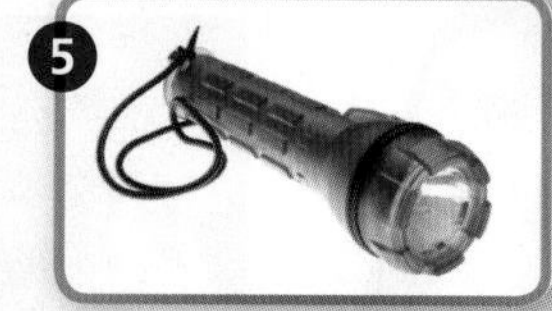
torch

6 
first aid kit

7 
towel

8 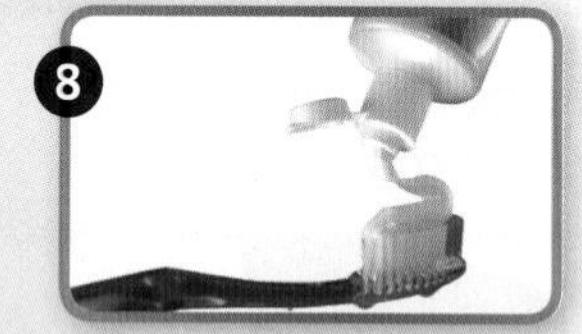
toothbrush and toothpaste

9 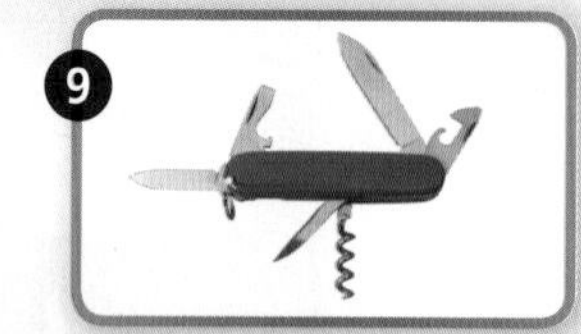
penknife

10 
map and compass

2 **Discuss with a partner. Write your ideas.** CD4 6 **Now listen and find out.**

I think he needs to take torch.

I agree. A torch is important. I don't think he needs to take a penknife.

3 CD4 7 **Listen and do the vocabulary quiz.**

This is big and flat. You put it on your bed when it's cold.

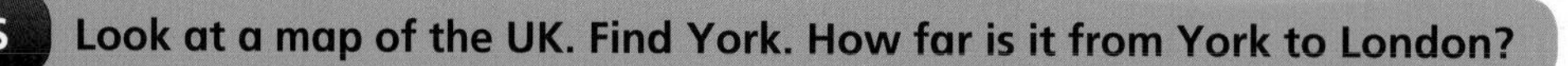

INTERNET TRACKS Look at a map of the UK. Find York. How far is it from York to London?

Lesson 2

POST ✓

We're at the campsite. It's in the Yorkshire Dales, near a big forest. The countryside is really beautiful! This is the list of the campsite rules. Do you think they are good rules?

4 Listen and read.

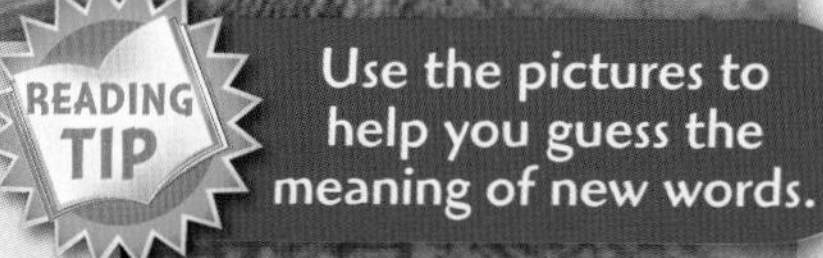

Use the pictures to help you guess the meaning of new words.

Welcome to the Yorkshire Dales Campsite.

Please read the list of rules.

Campsite rules

1. Please keep the campsite tidy. Do not drop litter. Use the bins and recycling bins.
2. Please do not make a noise, especially at night when people are asleep.
3. Do not play ball games in the tent area. You can play ball games on the sports field.
4. Do not make fires to cook. There is a barbecue area on the campsite where you can prepare food.
5. When you leave the campsite, always tell someone where you are going.
6. Please respect the forest and the countryside around the campsite.

Please follow these rules. They help us make the campsite a safe and happy place.

We hope you are going to have a fantastic holiday.

Mr Thompson

Director of the Yorkshire Dales Campsite

A B C

THINKING SKILLS
Remembering and memorising

5 Look at the pictures. Say the rules.

6 Play *Dictate and write*. Beat the clock.

Do not play ball games in the tent area.

7 Think and say.

'Please keep the campsite tidy.' This is a good rule because nobody wants to see litter on the campsite.

INTERNET TRACKS Find out what *Dales* means.

Lesson 3

8 Listen to and read the story.

POST
Hi everyone. I'm writing this from the campsite. This photo story is about an adventure we had yesterday. I hope you enjoy it.

The tiger thieves

- What have the tiger thieves got?
- Do the children catch the thieves?

The children are having breakfast at the campsite. They are talking about what they are going to do.

What are we going to do today?

Shhh! Listen to the radio.

Last night, a man and a woman took six tiger cubs from a wildlife park. The police believe they took the cubs to make a fur coat.

Later that day, Zoe, Scott and Florence hear a conversation.
The tiger cubs have got beautiful fur. And they've got stripes on their tails.
When are they going to arrive?
This afternoon at 3:20. A man is going to bring them to the campsite in a van.

9 **Read and answer the questions.**

1. How many tiger cubs are missing from the wildlife park?
2. What time is the van going to come to the campsite?
3. What do the children think is in the van?
4. Why do the man and woman want the toy tigers?
5. Are the man and woman angry with the children?
6. What are the children going to do with their toy tigers?

Tiger Time Values
Think about it!

Is it important to protect endangered species? Why?

What can you do to protect wildlife where you live?

7

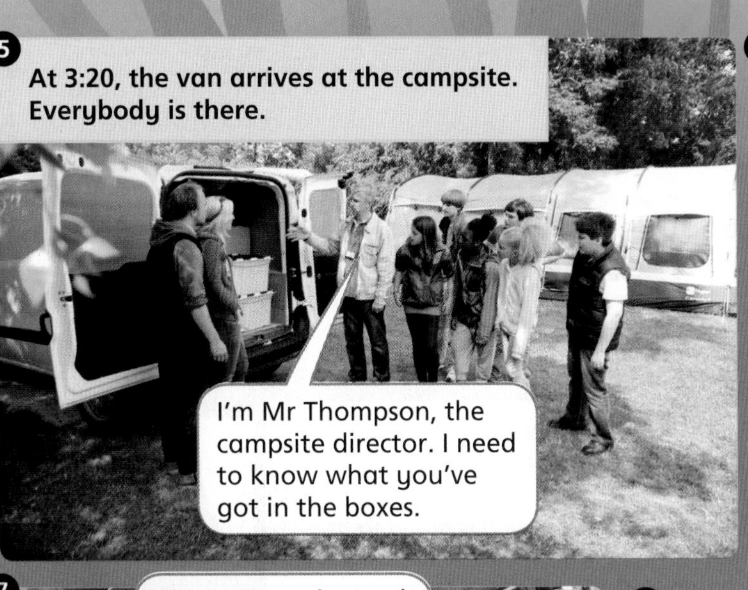
5
At 3:20, the van arrives at the campsite. Everybody is there.
I'm Mr Thompson, the campsite director. I need to know what you've got in the boxes.

6
We work for a charity called Save the Tigers. These toys are to help us promote the charity.
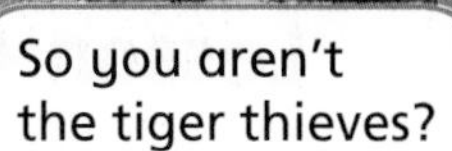
So you aren't the tiger thieves?

No, we aren't. We love tigers.

7

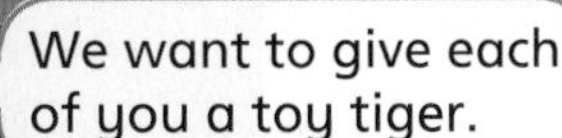
We want to give each of you a toy tiger.

Thank you. What a lovely souvenir of our holiday.

I'm glad you aren't the tiger thieves.

It doesn't matter. You were right to tell Mr Thompson.

8
Later, Mr Thompson takes a photo of the children.
With our tiger toys, we can help promote the charity. We can help save the tigers.
Good idea. I'm going to tell all my friends about it.
Hey! Listen to the radio.

9

Here is the news. Earlier today, the police caught the tiger thieves. The tiger cubs are back, with their mother, at the wildlife park.

Do you know...?

In the year 1900, there were approximately 100,000 tigers in the world. Today, there are less than 4,000.

10 Ask and say.

TALK ABOUT IT!

1 Do you like the story? Why? / Why not?
2 What's your favourite part of the story?
3 Do you think the children were right to tell Mr Thompson about the man and the woman?
4 Do you want to go on a camping trip in the UK?

Everyday phrases: learn and use!

That's an excellent idea!

Oh no! That's terrible.

I don't believe it!

It doesn't matter.

Lesson 4

11 CD4 11 **Listen and read. Is Becky worried about secondary school? Does Ed like his school?**

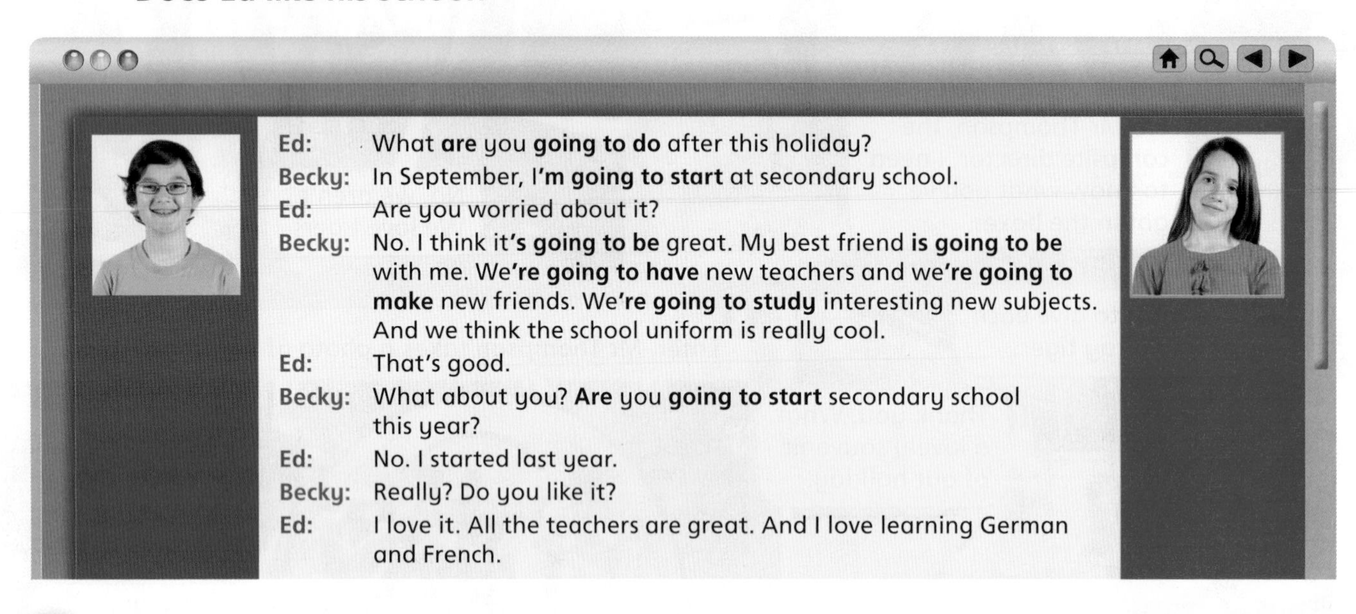

Ed: What **are** you **going to do** after this holiday?

Becky: In September, **I'm going to start** at secondary school.

Ed: Are you worried about it?

Becky: No. I think it**'s going to be** great. My best friend **is going to be** with me. We**'re going to have** new teachers and we**'re going to make** new friends. We**'re going to study** interesting new subjects. And we think the school uniform is really cool.

Ed: That's good.

Becky: What about you? **Are** you **going to start** secondary school this year?

Ed: No. I started last year.

Becky: Really? Do you like it?

Ed: I love it. All the teachers are great. And I love learning German and French.

12 **Act out the dialogue. Change the words to make it true for you.**

13 CD4 12 **Listen, repeat and learn.** digital

going to

I'm He's / She's You're / We're / They're	going to	study new subjects. make new friends. have new teachers.

I'm not He / She isn't You / We / They aren't	going to	study new subjects. make new friends. have new teachers.

Are you	going to	start secondary school?	Yes,	I am.	No,	I'm not.
Is he / she		wear a new uniform?		he / she is.		he / she isn't.

14 **Be a grammar detective! Look at page 67 in the AB.**

Do we use *going to* + verb to talk about the past or the future?

What verb do we always use before *going to*?

How many examples of *going to* + verb can you find in the story?

FAST TRACK GRAMMAR *Write five sentences about what you're going to do after school today.*

Lesson 5

Sound track
/ə/

15 Listen and identify. Listen and repeat.

What are you going to do today?

I'm going to read a book.

I'm going to take photos.

I'm going to walk the dog.

I'm going to play chess.

I'm going to watch a film.

I'm not going to do anything.

16 Listen and say *True* or *False*. Correct the false sentences.

	Saturday		Sunday	
Jack				
Jane				
Zach				
Annie				

17 Play *Who am I?*

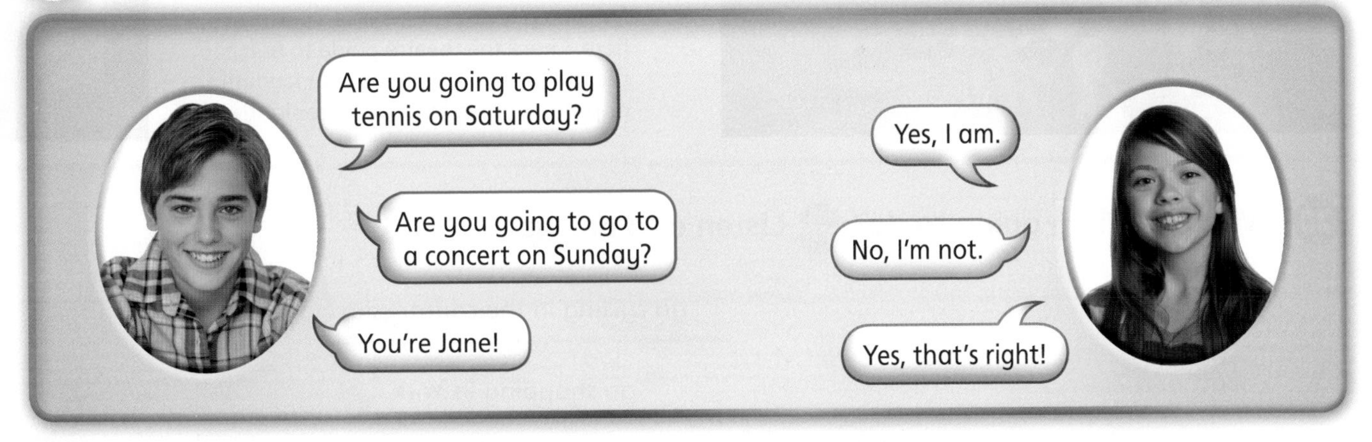
Are you going to play tennis on Saturday?
Yes, I am.
Are you going to go to a concert on Sunday?
No, I'm not.
You're Jane!
Yes, that's right!

18 Talk about you and your friends.

I'm going to play football tonight.
Toby is going to watch the football match.

TALK ABOUT IT!

FAST TRACK GRAMMAR *Write five sentences about your friends' plans for this weekend.*

Hello, everyone! Here's an excellent website that we're using to plan our holiday. Guess what we're going to do tomorrow.

POST

Cult

Lesson 6

19 Listen and read.

Things to do in Yorkshire

1 Do some sport in the Yorkshire Dales National Park
The National Park is an outdoor paradise for sporty people. There are paths where you can go trekking, cycling and horse riding. You can also go rock climbing, canoeing and sailing. But the best thing about the park is the beauty of the countryside. It's spectacular!

2 Travel by steam train
If you don't like trekking, a journey by steam train is a great way to see the Yorkshire countryside. You can see the beautiful hills and valleys from the comfort of your train.

3 Go shopping in York
The centre of York has got lots of excellent shops. It's the perfect place to buy your holiday souvenirs. And when you need a break, you can stop for a sandwich and a drink in a traditional café or a tearoom.

4 Visit York Castle Museum
Find out about life in the past through photos and exhibitions. Walk down a Victorian street to see how people lived 150 years ago. Go into the shops and talk to the people in Victorian costume. This fascinating museum is in the centre of York, in front of the castle. Check the museum's website for opening times and special exhibitions.

5 Spend a day at the Yorkshire Wildlife Park
Lions, lemurs, parrots and lizards – there are animals from all around the world in the park. You can also see one of the rarest species of tiger in the world: the Siberian tiger. All the animals live in big open spaces in the park and visitors can see them from the footpaths.

6 Visit Yorkshire Sculpture Park
If you like walking and you like art, this is the place for you. Walk around the park to see more than 60 sculptures in the beautiful landscape. There are also exhibitions in five indoor galleries. There is a restaurant, a café and a souvenir shop. Check the park's website for opening times and special events.

7 See a play or a pop concert
Yorkshire has got lots of theatres. Pop, film and television stars often perform here. Check the theatre guide to find a theatre near you. Perhaps your favourite pop star is going to perform tonight!

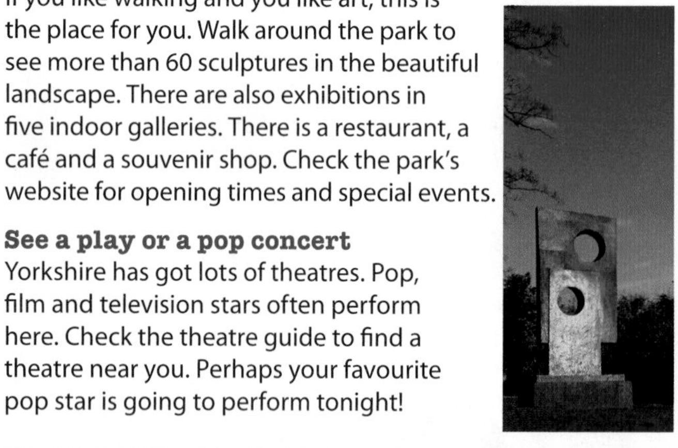

20 What are they going to do? Listen and answer.

- Scott and Zoe
- Ed and Finn
- Becky and Florence

are going to

- go cycling in the countryside
- go shopping in York
- visit the museum
- travel by steam train
- go to a pop concert

tomorrow.

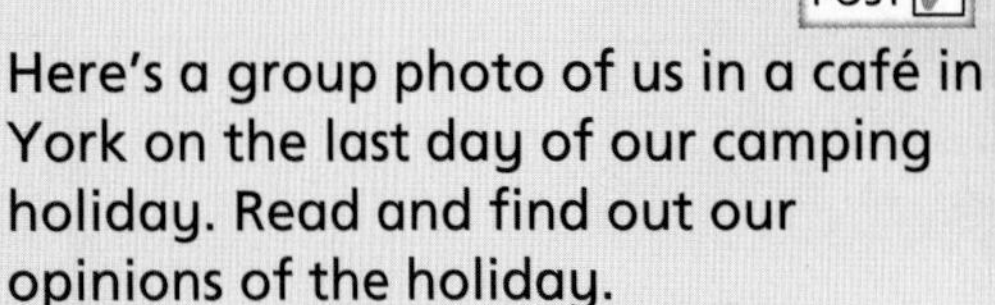

Here's a group photo of us in a café in York on the last day of our camping holiday. Read and find out our opinions of the holiday.

Lesson 7

21 Listen and read.

What were their favourite places in Yorkshire?
Which activities did they enjoy doing?

One day, we travelled by steam train. I think old trains are fantastic, so that was my favourite activity. And the most interesting place was the sculpture park. I really like art. I think some of the sculptures were amazing. Really cool.

The best activity for me was rock climbing in the National Park. I had a really good instructor and we climbed for three hours. The most interesting place for me was York. There were so many amazing buildings and things to look at. It's a beautiful city.

I liked all the places we visited. But number one for me was the beautiful old shopping streets in York. I love shopping! And my favourite activity was cooking at the campsite. I helped prepare some of the meals. It was fun.

I really enjoyed cycling in the countryside. Yorkshire is very green. The views are spectacular. My favourite place? I think it was the wildlife park. We saw some awesome animals, especially the big cats. They all looked really healthy and happy.

I really enjoyed trekking in the countryside because Yorkshire is so beautiful. The views are incredible. But my favourite place was the Castle Museum in York. I love history, so it was really interesting. It was amazing to see how life was in the past.

One evening, we saw a concert at an open-air theatre. I think that was my favourite activity. I didn't know the pop group, but their music was great. And I think my favourite place was the campsite. I loved it. It was lots of fun. The drama with the tiger cub toys was exciting, too. And now we've all got fantastic souvenirs!

TALK ABOUT IT!

22 Listen and say *True* or *False*. Correct the false sentences.

23 Say where you want to go and what you want to do in Yorkshire.

I want to go shopping in York and see the Castle Museum.

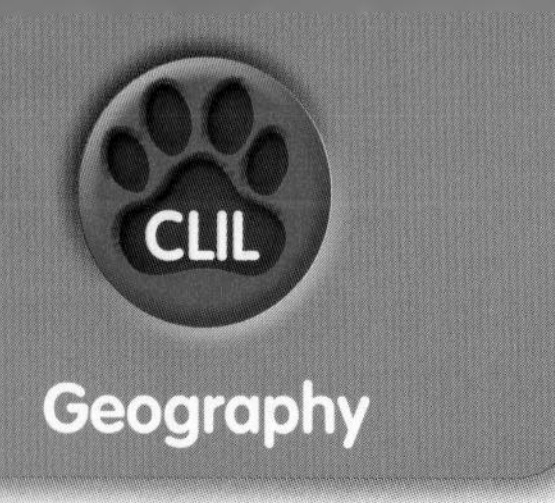

Geography

Lesson 8

24 Listen and read.

The weather forecast was very important during our holiday in Yorkshire, so I'm posting this article about weather stations and weather forecasts. Do you know who writes the weather forecast? Read and find out. POST

What do meteorologists do?

Meteorologists study the weather. They receive information from weather stations about changes in temperature, air pressure, wind and rain. They also study images of the Earth from satellites. The meteorologists use this information to understand how our climate works, and to write weather forecasts.

What are weather forecasts?

Weather forecasts tell us what the weather is going to be like. Many people listen to weather forecasts on the radio or on television. You can also find weather forecasts online or in newspapers.

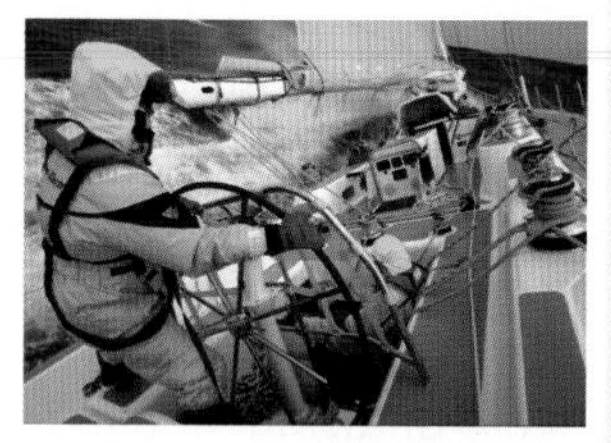

The weather forecast can help everyone make simple decisions such as what to wear, or where to go at the weekend. But for some people, the weather forecast is very, very important. Pilots and sailors need to know about storms and strong winds before they can travel. Farmers need to know about rain, heatwaves and hailstorms to protect their animals and crops. Foresters and firefighters need to know about heatwaves to prevent and put out forest fires.

Thunder and lightning

Lightning is electricity that comes from a storm cloud. It's extremely hot. It's hotter than the surface of the sun! Thunder is the sound of air moving very quickly. It happens when lightning strikes.

Heatwaves

A heatwave is when the temperatures are higher than normal for a long period of time.

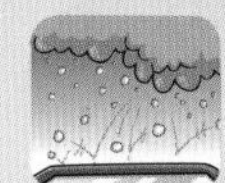

Hailstorms

In a hailstorm, small balls of ice fall from the sky. Sometimes, the balls of ice can be bigger than golf balls!

Tornados

A tornado is a column of spinning air. The top touches storm clouds and the bottom touches the ground. Tornados can move at more than 300km an hour.

25 Read and answer.

1. What do meteorologists study?
2. What else do meteorologists do?
3. Where can you read a weather forecast?
4. Who needs to know about…
   - heatwaves
   - thunder storms
   - tornados
   - hailstorms

26 Play *Association*.

THINKING SKILLS
Associating

Lightning.
It's extremely hot.
It's electricity.
It's frightening.

27 Think and say.

My world

What's the weather like today?

Are there sometimes tornados, storms and heatwaves where you live?

My words to remember

hailstorm thunder lightning
weather forecast tornado heatwave

Find out the size of the biggest hailstone in history.

Project: Planning a weekend away

 **28** Listen and read.

I'm going to go away for the weekend with my mum. This is what we're going to do. Do you like our plans?

POST ✓

What I'm going to do

Next weekend, I'm going to go to Edinburgh with my mother. We're going to take the train from Manchester on Friday after school. It leaves at quarter to five. It arrives in Edinburgh at half past eight. The journey takes nearly four hours, so we're going to take books to read on the train. And we're going to take sandwiches and drinks.

In Edinburgh, we're going to stay with my aunt, my mother's sister. We're going to visit Edinburgh castle on Saturday morning. After that, we're going to go shopping in the city centre. I want to buy some earrings. In the evening, we're going to see a play at the theatre.

On Sunday we're going to walk in the botanical garden before lunch. Then, in the afternoon, we're going to catch the train back to Manchester.

The weather forecast says that it's going to be cloudy but it isn't going to rain. I think we're going to have a fantastic weekend!

By Becky

Train ticket
From:
Manchester
Ticket type:
Standard weekend return
To:
Edinburgh
Ticket number:
00123987

29 Plan your project.

THINKING SKILLS
Planning

1. Decide where to go and how to get there.
2. Decide what you're going to do at your destination.
3. Check the weather forecast.
4. Write and present your plans.

You can also present your project in this way.

➜ AB page 72

Do the Unit 7 Review and Self-assessment (Activity Book page 72). Complete your *Progress Journal* for Unit 7.

World Music Day

1 Listen and read.

Hi, everyone! World Music Day is a celebration of music all over the world. This website tells you about how we celebrate World Music Day in the UK! I hope you like it.

POST

What is World Music Day?

World Music Day is a festival on 21st June every year. It started in France over thirty years ago. Some people wanted to have a special day when everyone could listen to music. All the events in the festival were free. The musicians didn't have to pay for a place to perform. They could play anywhere – inside a building or outside on the street!

Today, this festival is popular in many countries around the world. Many musicians want to play their music on this day. But there are two important rules. The first rule is that the festival has to be on 21st June – this is Midsummer's Day in the UK. The second rule is that all events must be free so anyone can take part, and anyone can watch.

Many bands and musicians play music all night! And there is music for everyone – from classical music to rap and jazz.

Do you celebrate World Music Day in your country? Where do you like to listen to music?

2 Listen and read. Sing.

Hello again! This year, for World Music Day, we are going to listen to a special song!

POST

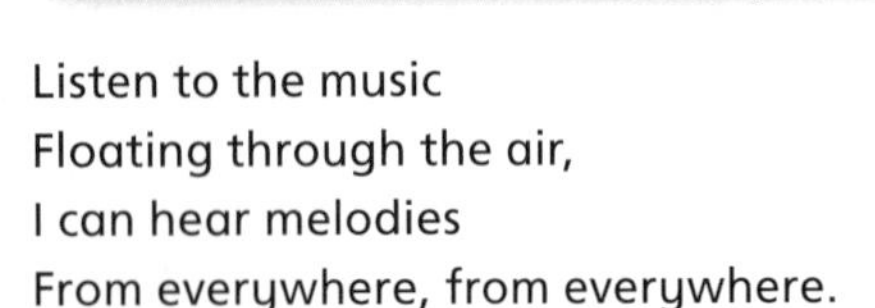

Listen to the music
Floating through the air,
I can hear melodies
From everywhere, from everywhere.

Look at the musicians
Dressed in black and white,
Listen to them play
All through the night.

Listen to the music
Floating through the air,
I can hear clapping
From everywhere, from everywhere,

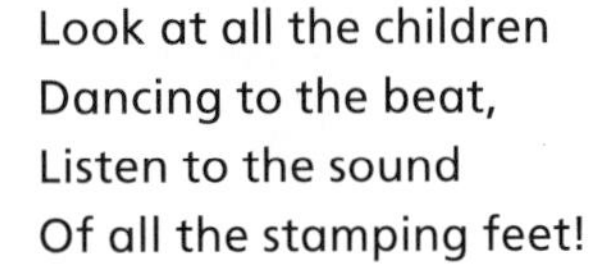

Look at all the children
Dancing to the beat,
Listen to the sound
Of all the stamping feet!

Listen to the music
Floating through the air,
I can feel the rhythms
From everywhere, from everywhere.

Inventor's Day

1 CD4 27 **Listen and read.**

Hi there! In the UK and USA, people celebrate Inventor's Day on 11th February every year. This is one of my favourite days because at school we make our own inventions! Here's an excellent website where you can find out all about it. POST

The origins of Inventor's Day

Inventor's Day is on 11th February. This is the date when Thomas Edison was born in 1847. He was a brilliant American scientist and he invented many different objects. Today we still use many of these objects. His most famous invention was an electric light bulb.

New inventions, like the light bulb, made people's lives easier and better. Some of the first inventions were thousands of years ago, for example, the wheel.

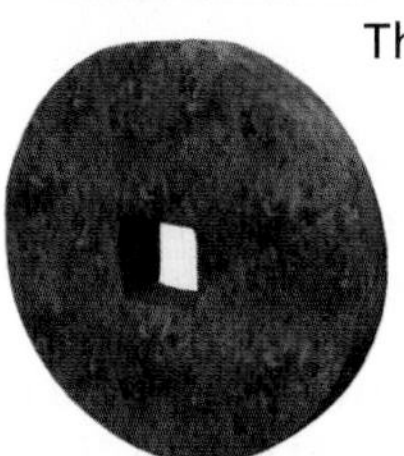

The wheel was a very important invention because it helped people travel from one place to another, to carry heavy loads and to make pottery. Today, cars, buses, trains, planes and bikes all use the wheel. Can you imagine life without these things?

People invented many other machines and objects a long time ago, like paper, pottery, glass and cloth. We still use these inventions today. Can you think of other examples?

Inventions today

Some inventions can also cause problems. For example, many machines use raw materials like coal, gas and wood. These resources are running out and they can also cause pollution. Many inventors today are trying to invent objects and machines that use resources that do not pollute the air, like solar power.

How do you celebrate Inventor's Day in your country? What important inventors or inventions do you know?

2 CD4 28 **Listen and read. Make a special invention.**

Hi! We made an invention at school today. We used beans, some plastic food wrap and a plastic pot. Can you guess what our invention is? This is how to make it! POST

How to make a percussion instrument

You need:
- a clean, empty yoghurt pot or plastic food container
- some plastic food wrap
- a marker pen
- a large rubber band
- scissors
- some dry rice or beans

What to do
1. Cut off a piece of plastic food wrap.
2. Put the pot or container face-down on the plastic food wrap.
3. Draw around the shape of the pot or container, 8cm from the edge.
4. Cut out the shape you drew on the plastic food wrap.
5. Put the rice or beans into the container.
6. Stretch the plastic food wrap tightly over the end of the container and hold it in place with the rubber band.
7. Shake your percussion instrument to make a sound!

Independence Day

1  **Listen and read.**

Hi there! In Mexico, 16th September is a very important day. It's Independence Day! Here's a blog to tell you all about it! POST

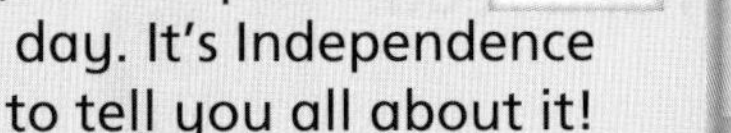

Mexican Independence Day

Over two hundred years ago, Mexico was a Spanish colony. The Spanish government ruled the country, but the people living in Mexico didn't like the Spanish government. Life was hard for many Mexicans. They thought there were too many laws and these laws took away their freedom.

In 1810, many people in Mexico decided they wanted to be an independent country.

They fought for a long time against the Spanish. Eleven years later, in 1821, Mexico was free from Spain and became an independent nation.

Today, Mexicans all over the world celebrate Mexican Independence Day on 16th September. The celebrations begin before midnight on 15th September, when the president says 'El Grito' in the main square in Mexico City, the capital. During this speech he talks about the heroes of the independence, and finishes by saying 'Viva Mexico!' three times. Lots of people watch this on television and, the next day, there are parades all over the country. People wear traditional costumes and decorate their homes and cars with Mexican flags. Thousands of people come to Mexico City. During the parades, bands play music and people wave flags. Everyone has a good time. After, many families celebrate with food and songs. There are also concerts and fireworks.

Do you have a national day or a special day that you celebrate every year in your country? When is it?

2  **Listen and read. Make a golden eagle.**

Hello! Did you know that the national bird of Mexico is the golden eagle? This beautiful bird is North America's largest bird of prey. Would you like to make your own golden eagle? Here is how to make it. POST

How to make a golden eagle

You need:
- the eagle template
- scissors
- paints, crayons or coloured pens
- glue

What to do

1 Cut out the eagle template.
2 Colour or paint your eagle. Colour the head light brown and the beak yellow and white.
3 Colour or paint the top part of the wings dark brown and the bottom part light brown and white.
4 Colour the body dark brown.
5 Colour the claws orange and the tail black and white.
6 Roll the eagle's body into a cylinder and stick the ends together.
7 Stick on the head, wings, claws and tail.

Fabulous!

Songs bank

Everyone's welcome at our youth club

I like running, climbing. I love scuba diving.
My sister likes painting, writing and designing.
My brother likes playing the clarinet.
I've got a friend. He likes using the internet.

Chorus
Musical, technical, scientific,
Adventurous, sporty or artistic.
We're all different, that's OK.
We don't want to be the same.
Everyone's welcome at our youth club.
Our super cool, very cool after school youth club.
Everyone's welcome at our youth club.

I like juggling, swimming. I love going fishing.
My sister likes reading, singing and just thinking.
My brother likes playing basketball,
And I've got a friend. She doesn't like sport at all.

Chorus

My superhero

Some superheroes can climb mountains high.
Some superheroes can fly in the sky.
Some can jump across the seas.
Some can save the forests and the trees.

My best friend cannot climb.
He isn't strong. He cannot fly.
But my best friend is very kind.
He's the kindest, most generous person I know.
My best friend is my superhero!
My super, super superhero!

Some superheroes can catch waterfalls.
Some superheroes can crash into walls.
Some can lift a thousand kilos.
Some can stop erupting volcanoes.

My best friend cannot climb.
She isn't strong. She cannot fly.
But my best friend is very kind.
She's the kindest, most generous person I know.
My best friend is my superhero!
My super, super superhero!

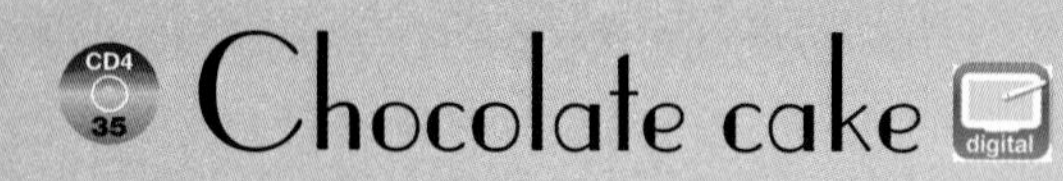

Chocolate cake

Let's bake,
Let's bake.
Let's make a cake.
A cake for friends and family.
A cake we can have with a cup of tea.
A cup of tea.

There's some flour,
There are eggs,
There's some sugar and spice.
There's some butter and ***chocolate***,
Mmmm! That's very nice.

Put it in a bowl,
Mix it with a spoon,
Put it in the oven,
And very, very soon, you've got a ***chocolate*** cake.
A ***chocolate*** cake.
Yeah! Everybody loves a ***chocolate*** cake.
Mmmm! Delicious.

*(Repeat, replacing **chocolate** with **coffee**)*

WHO'S GOT THE STATUE?

THE DAILY NEWS

STATUE MISSING

At ten past three yesterday afternoon the statue of the king was in the centre of the square. At twenty past three, the statue was missing. Where were you at quarter past three yesterday afternoon? Did you see the robbery? Do you know who has got the statue?

Chorus
Who's got the statue?
Who? Who? Who?
Did you take the statue?
Was it you, you or you?

It wasn't me.
I wasn't there.
I was nowhere near the square.
I was at the theme park at quarter past three.
You can ask my sister.
She was there with me.

Chorus

It wasn't me.
I wasn't there.
I was nowhere near the square.
I was at the airport at quarter past three.
You can ask my brother.
He was there with me.

Chorus

 Inventions, inventions 

Chorus
Inventions, inventions, some are truly great.
The microwave, the dictionary and the rollerskate.
Inventions, inventions, some are truly hip.
The microscope, the microphone and the paperclip.

What did Graham Bell invent?
Was it something great?
Where did he invent it?
And do you know the date?

Chorus

What did Roland Hill invent?
Was it something great?
Where did he invent it?
And do you know the date?

Chorus

What did Orville Wright invent?
Was it something great?
Where did he invent it?
And do you know the date?

Chorus

 We're gonna go camping 

Chorus
We're gonna go camping in the country.
We're gonna sleep in a tent tonight.
We're gonna go camping in the country.
We're gonna have fun on a campsite.

I'm packing a penknife. I'm packing a rope,
Toothbrush and toothpaste and some soap.
I think I've got everything I'm gonna need.
Don't forget to take a book to read.

Chorus

I'm packing a blanket. I'm packing my shoes,
Sunglasses, sun cream and shampoo.
I think I've got everything. I've got it all.
Don't forget to take a bat and ball.

Chorus

I'm packing a compass. I'm packing a map,
Waterproof jacket and a cap.
I think I've got everything. I think that's it.
Don't forget to take a first aid kit.

Chorus

gonna = going to

Macmillan Education
4 Crinan Street
London N1 9XW
A division of Macmillan Publishers Limited

Companies and representatives throughout the world

ISBN 978-0-230-48381-1
Pack ISBN 978-0-230-48415-3

This edition published 2015
First edition entitled "Tiger Tracks" published 2014 by Macmillan Publishers Limited

Original design by Blooberry Design Ltd
Page make-up by Andrew Magee Design Ltd
Illustrated by David Belmonte (Beehive), Humberto Blanco (Sylvie Poggio), Jerome Brasseur (Beehive), Emmanuel Cerisier (Beehive), Kevin Hopgood (Beehive), Martin Impey, Andy Parker, Anthony Rule, Victor Tavares (Beehive)
Cover design by Astwood Design Consultancy
Cover photographs by Corbis, Getty, Stuart Cox, Photodisk, Stockbyte
Songs produced and arranged by Tom, Dick and Debbie Productions
Recordings produced and arranged by RBA Productions
Pictures researched by Victoria Gaunt

Authors' acknowledgements
We would like to thank everyone at Macmillan Education in the UK and in Spain who has helped us in the development and the production of these materials. We would also like to thank all the teachers who have taken time to read, pilot and give feedback at every stage of writing the course. Special thanks from Carol to Alan, Jamie and Hannah for their encouragement and support. Special thanks from Mark to Carlos for his patience and understanding.

Acknowledgments
The publishers would like to thank the following teachers:
Amparo Fernández Ortiz, CEIP La Patacona, Alboraya, Valencia; Anna Esteban Nieto, Escola Jaume Ferran I Clua, Valldoreix, Barcelona; Carlota López Petidier, CEIP Miguel de Cervantes, Torrejón de Ardoz, Madrid; María del Mar Rodríguez Rodríguez, Escola Els Pins, Barcelona; Mª Inmaculada Cercadillo Torrecilla, CEIP Gabriel García Márquez, Getafe, Madrid; Paco Sansaloni Felis, CEIP Cervantes, Gandía, Valencia; Patricia Meneses Dekker, Escola Esteve Barrachina, Sitges, Barcelona; Teresa Rofes Bauzá, Escola Barcelona, Barcelona.

The authors and publishers would like to thank the following for permission to reproduce their photographs:

Alamy/Andrew Aitchison p34(4), Alamy/Blend Images p74(tc), Alamy/Bon Appetit p30(cr), Alamy/The Art Archive p45(tcl), Alamy/Prisma Bildagentur AG p15(waterfall), Alamy/blickwinkel p30(cmr), Alamy/PearlBucknall p64(1), Alamy/David Colbran p43(insert), Alamy/Ian Dagnall pp73(tcr,insert), Alamy/eye35 p34(8), Alamy/Gaertner p62(bcr), Alamy/Juniors Bildarchiv GmbH p20(3), Alamy/David Hastilow p50(tm), Alamy/Helga p64(5), Alamy/ Louise Heusinkveld p20(2), Alamy/Steffan Hill p74(b), Alamy/Cindy Hopkins p14(9), Alamy/D. Hurst pp44(7), 64(10), Alamy/Imagestate p14(8), Alamy/Kuttig—RF—Kids p5(cl), Alamy/Art Kowalsky p14(3), Alamy/Andrew Linscott p70(cr), Alamy/Loop Images Ltd p70(bl), Alamy/MITO Images p74 (tr), Alamy/Keith Morris p10(cl), Alamy/Sean O'Neill p55(bcr), Alamy/scenicireland.com/Christopher Hill Photographic p35(bcr), Alamy/David R. Frazier Photolibrary, Inc p34(7), Alamy/Craig Joiner Photography p34(10), Alamy/Colin Palmer Photography p34(9), Alamy/Big Cheese Photo LLC p62(tcr), Alamy/Buzz Pictures p72(tcr), Alamy/Aliaksandr Mazurkevich p44(5), Alamy/MBI p74(tcl), Alamy/Jeff Morgan 05 p34(6), Alamy/Realimage p44(2), Alamy/Rtimages p64(8), Alamy/ Richard Semik p70(cl), Alamy/Frans Lanting Studio p20(1), Alamy/Superstock p14(4), Alamy/Eye Ubiquitous p44(10), Alamy/A.P.S (UK) p11(stadium), Alamy/Finnbarr Webster p45(bcr); **Brand X Pictures** p14(10); **COMSTOCK IMAGES** p30(cm); **Corbis** pp32(cl), 64(9), Corbis/a.collectionRF/amanaimages p24(5), Corbis/Heide Benser p9(l), 15(bl), 35(l), 42(bl), 48(bl), 52(bl), 59(l), 72(bl), Corbis/Bettmann p49(tm), Corbis/Joe Toth/BPI p11(footballer), Corbis/Hulton-Deutsch Collection pp45(bcl), 79(tr), Corbis/Hero Images Inc p55 (c), Corbis/Kang Kim/Gallery Stock/Galeries p32(cr), Corbis/Joe Toth/BPI p11(footballer), Corbis/Matthias Hiekel/dpa p10(cm), Corbis/KidStock/Blend Images pp9(r), 15(br), 35(r), 42(br), 48(br), 52(br), 59(r), 72(br), Corbis/Radius Images p15(cr), Corbis/TEK IMAGE/Science Photo Library p64(6), Corbis/Wieder, Frank/the food passionates p24(9), Corbis/Lew Robertson p24(10), Corbis/Creativ Studio Heinemann/Westend61 p24(1), Corbis/Steve Vidler p34(2), **FLPA**/Mike Perry/Minden Pictures p18(cr); **Getty Images** pp24(4, 8), Getty Images pp35(cr), 60(tcr, cl, bcl, cr), 61(tcr), 79(tl), 79(tm), Getty Images/AFP p34(3), 72(tcl), Getty Images/Hulton Archive p53(tcl), Getty Images/Alistair Berg p5(cr), Getty Images/Mark Bowden p62(tcl), Getty Images/Zero Creatives p5(bcl), Getty Images/Creative Crop p31(cmr), Getty Images/Thierry Dosogne p34(5), Getty Images/Vladimir Godnik p42(tcl), Getty Images/Rick Gomez pp2(bl),8(cl),12(br),19(bl), 25(bl), 39(l), 45(bl), 52(bl), 55(br), 62(br), 69(l), Getty Images/Steve Gorton p64(2), Getty Images/Robert Harding p14(2), Getty Images/Travel Ink p41(tcl), Getty Images/Juanmonino p30(tcl), Getty Images/Kristin Lee p24(2), Getty Images/Doug McKinlay p35(tcr), Getty Images/Jose Moya p50(tl), Getty Images/Maximilian Stock Ltd p24(3), Getty Images/Robert Decelis Ltd p60(c), Getty Images/Stuart Pearce p8(tr), Getty Images/Time & Life Pictures p52(bcl), Getty Images/Yellowdog Productions p62(bcl), Getty Images/Referns p11(concert), Getty Images/Sami Sarkis p63(insert), Getty Images/Image Source pp5(bcr), 24(7), Getty Images/ Bluemoon Stock p64(4), Getty Images/Lucidio Studio, Inc. p32(cm), Getty Images/Maria Teijeiro p21(tcr), Getty Images/David Tipling p21(cr), Getty Images/UIG p50(cl), Getty Images/Tom Pfeiffer/VolcanoDiscovery p14(1), Getty Images/Ingmar Wesemann p14(5), Getty Images/yellowdog p55(bcl); **Guinness World Records** p18(tl); **Image 100** p30(cl); **Imagesource** pp18(tr), 42(bcl, bcm), 44(6), 63(tm, tr), Image Source/Corbis pp47, 50(cm), 52(bcr), Image Source/Moodboard p34(1); **Photo courtesy of Johnson & Johnson** p49(tl); **Macmillan Australia** p64(7); **Macmillan Publishers/Stuart Cox** pp3(cl), 4, 6, 10(t), 10(b), 11(t), p12(t), 13(t), 14(tl), 16, 20(tl, b), 21(t), 23(t), 24(tl), 24(6), 25(t), 30(t, b), 31(t), 32(t), 33(t), 34(t), 35(t), 36(t), 40(t, b), 41(t), 42(t), 43(t), 44(t), 45(t), 46, 50(t), 50(bm), 51(tm), 52(t), 53(t), 54, 55(t), 55(tcl), 56, 60(t), 60(bm), 61(t), 62(tm), 63(tl), 64(t), 65(t), 66(t), 68(r, l), 70(t), 71(t), 72(t), 73(t), 74(t), 74(bcm), 75(tcl, bcm), 76(cr,b); **Photograph courtesy of Mark Ormerod** p25(cake); **Photodisc** p33(cr); **Photoshot**/Martin Ciesielski p25(palm), Photoshot/The Irish Image Collection p40(cr), Photoshot/UPPA p48(tm), Photoshot/ChinaFotoPress/Gu Yue p53(tcl, insert); **REX**/Canadian Press p60(bcr); **Royal Mail** p61(bcr); **Science Source** p45(tcr); **Sherlock Holmes Museum** p41(tcr); **Stockbyte** p44(3); **Superstock**/Eye Ubiquitous p76(tl), Superstock/Food and Drink p30(bcl), SuperStock/Blend Images pp2(br), 8(cr), 12(bl), 19(br), 25(br), 39(r), 45(bl), 49(br), 55(bl), 62(bl), 69(r), Superstock/Axiom Photographic/Design Pics p75(b), Superstock/Pixtal p52 (tcm), Superstock/Stockbroker/Purestock p51(tr), Superstock/Superstock p75 (tl); **Thinkstock**/BananaStock p10(cr), Thinkstock/JaySi p5(bcl), Thinkstock/Jupiterimages p74(tl), Thinkstock/OlgaMiltsova p31(c); Thinkstock/Purestock p8(tl), Thinkstock/istock pp14(6, 7), 19(tl, tr), 31(t), 42(tcm), 44(1), 44(4), 44(8), 64(3), Thinkstock/Photodisc p19(tml), Thinkstock/Pixand p42(tcr), Thinkstock/Ryan McVay p74 (tr), Thinkstock/Stockbyte p19(tmr); Thinkstock/Valua Vitaly p74(t); Thinkstock/**Up the Resolution** p30(tcl); **Wham-O** p49(tr); **Yorkshire Sculpture Park**/Barbara Hepworth, Squares With Two Circles, 1963. Courtesy Tate © Bowness, Hepworth Estate. Photo © Jonty Wilde p70(br).
Commissioned photography by Stuart Cox: pp2(t, c), 4(tl, tr, b), 5(b), 11(bl, br), 13(cr, cl), 21(bcr), 23(cl), 31(b), 33(b), 41(br, bl), 43(b), 51(br), 53(br), 61(br), 63(br), 65(b), 66(1—4), 67(5—9), 71(b), 73(br), 79(br, bl).
Author photograph (Carol Read) by Michael Selley
Thanks to Edward, Brandon, Kellah, James, Lola and Ophia.

Printed and bound in Spain

2019 2018 2017 2016
10 9 8 7 6 5 4